All Nature Speaks

CONVERSATIONS WITH PETS & WILDLIFE

NANCY ORLEN WEBER

Unlimited Mind

Publications

Lightwing Center
P.O. Box 1132
Denville, NJ 07834
https://nancyorlenweber.com/
nancy@nancyorlenweber.com

Contact the publisher through Lightwingcenter@gmail.com Subject: All Nature Speaks

ISBN: 978-1-66781-041-6 for printed book.
ISBN: 978-1-66781-042-3 for ebook.

Signed soft cover and hard cover books only available at
https://nancyorlenweber.com/

Some names were changed to protect the persons' privacy.

Design, final editing and formatting by BookBaby.com.
Photos and Art by Nancy Orlen Weber.
Logo for Unlimited Mind Publishing by Julie Bond Genovese.
Back Cover Photo by Greg Martz

Introduction

I am not an expert on horses, cats, dogs, flies, snakes, trees, flowers, humans, stones, mountains, water, air, fire, or pretty much any created object. I am a living being, an embodiment of life. I practice connecting with the essence of love, to ease the pain, the hurt, the bewilderment, the confusion, of another being, with the hope and prayer that we both benefit.

A shy childhood, where I thought of myself as invisible, helped me discover that other life forms accepted me. I made friends with a colony of ants outside the doors of our East 45th Street, Brooklyn home. Watching their kinship and teamwork, I wondered if other life forms, like bushes, trees, and flowering plants, also loved and helped each other. Thus began my love affair with all of life.

Now regarded as an animal/insect/plant communicator, I have been sought out by people who also know they talk with (not to) their pets, wildlife, trees, plants, and more. All life communicates at some level. The same vital energy that animates a tree also flows through us.

While I have made attempts to learn other languages, Spanish comes a bit easier (not much) than others. It has been easier for me to "talk" with a groundhog or a chipmunk than to learn another human language. I hope that the stories you are about to read of soul-to-soul experiences with other beings inspires you to continue your love of, and for, communion with all other sentient beings.

My wish is for all of us to see life as the extraordinary art of our Creator. As you continue to build loving relationships with all other creatures of this world, may you feel the faith, love, and trust that happens when we experience the invisible world of heart-talk.

In the Infinite Light of Love,

– Nancy Orlen Weber

The clearest way into the Universe is through a forest wilderness.

– John Muir

Foreword

Thirty-six years ago, I never dreamt that my life and career would be where it is today. As an aspiring concert pianist, I also had an intense love of animals. When it came down to choosing between my love of music, and the animals, I decided to merge my love of the outdoors and animals into a career. Veterinary medicine offered me that opportunity. After ten years practicing traditional veterinary medicine, I suffered a potentially career-ending injury. As it would happen, I had witnessed significant differences in some of my patients, when they received chiropractic and acupuncture treatments from a colleague. Everyone has an "aha" moment, when an experience makes everything crystal clear, so I sought these options for my own healing. Thus began my journey, melding holistic methods with traditional treatments, not only for my own health but for my patients and clients as well.

Doors to other amazing worlds opened, as I learned about options for health and healing. Energy medicine comes in many forms, including *acknowledging intuitive aspects of each, that often may not have a full physical explanation. I was taken back to my days of music lessons and performing, when I learned about the healing properties of frequency. Using sound and essential oils because of their frequencies, is now routine in my veterinary practice, to facilitate true healing on different levels in a synergistic manner.*

Perhaps the biggest revelation in my life's path, has been learning (or re-learning) that there is something inside that should be recognized, listened to, and nurtured. One of my favorite gifts as a kid was the Kreskin's ESP Board Game. My brothers thought I had some way of "cheating" the system. I didn't know how I did it, I just knew…and did. Somewhere along the way, we seem to lose the ability, to use that part of ourselves in a meaningful fashion. It's an honor to work with mentors like Nancy. How truly inspiring to learn we can expand this innate God-given talent that resides in all of us. Her work and guidance continue to benefit so many humans and animals. As you follow Nancy's journey, know that everyone comes to the place they are meant to be, at just the right time. There is an understanding that often words cannot express. Staying present with love in your heart, will enable you to trust yourself and BE. Learn from Nancy's experiences, and look forward to exciting new chapters in your own life with the animals of the world. ENJOY!!

Susan Albright, DVM

Dedication

Each species is a masterpiece, a creation assembled
with extreme care and genius. —Edward O. Wilson

This book is dedicated to Sweetie Pi R squared, born of a Bronx Jewish Deli gray striped feline guy, who fell in love with a Puerto Rican feline beauty in the Spanish grocery store on 161st street and the Grand Concourse in Bronx, New York. She was one hour old when we met, lying in her mother's front paws, cuddled like a beloved child should be. Sweetie Pi slept on my pillow for 18 dreamy years. When my husband Dick entered my life, he also embraced this feisty, spiritual feline who accepted both of us as her companions providing she had first dibs on the bed. She now escorts other departed souls into the nonmaterial planes.

After Sweetie Pi's departure from earth, Boo Girl, a feline feral rescue, finally slept on the bed and at twelve years of age broke through her own fears and began introducing herself to all our friends. Boo Girl will explain everything later in the book. To all the canines who let me share their joy at living (most were rescues), all the ants I played with as a child, Fifi LaPew, Rocky Racoon, and all in between, thank you for being my teachers. You teach me to believe in the Creator of all life, showing me again and again that love does conquer fear.

To my children Rebecca and Jesse, who spent hours helping rescue animals feel safe, and now each has their own menagerie; you have always inspired me to trust love. To all my students and clients who brought me their problems with animals, and to all those animals for the last fifty years who have allowed me to work with them, I thank you all for trusting me to help. May I always live up to that trust.

Dream Bird

To the best crazy partner our Creator conjured up for me, my beloved Dickens. I love and adore you. You bring out the best and the worst in me. As you said, "marriage is freedom." I am free in your presence to do what I have been called to do. Thank you, my love.

TABLE OF CONTENTS

Chapter 1

My First Teachers of Heart-Talk

This little girl was from Brooklyn, with cracks in the pavement to watch. Ants have little girls watching them live in the cracks, build their homes, help their friends, and if they like her, a trip up her arm. That's what I recall when I think of my earliest experiences with other species.

I could sit and watch this miniature world, and have them lightly tickle me for hours. Being around the ants taught me how one species could trust another. There is always that little girl inside me, talking, remembering, and thinking how big I must appear, how loud my steps must sound. Most days, before stepping outside, I call out in my mind to all the creatures, to warn them, that this bigger-than-them being is about to enter their world. That to me, is heart talk. A simple way to thank and acknowledge every being, for sharing this beautiful planet with me.

Every year my sister, mom, dad, and I would visit my maternal grandmother in New Hampshire. My father took us out to pick blueberries in the woods nearby and then have a little picnic. There was a stream about ten feet from our blanket where we sat and ate. I was never one to enjoy sitting still for long. While they were still eating, I jumped up and crossed over the stream. A pretty little red puppy came over to me and we played. I was petting her/him when my father stood looking from the other side of the stream and shouted "Nancy!"

"Daddy, I want to keep this puppy. I love her."

The puppy ran as soon as my father yelled. I was crying when he said, "That's not a puppy! That's a fox!"

I can still feel the sweet fox's fur, and my joy at the instant kinship.

I am always looking to improve my communication with the rest of the world. I have a ritual that takes anywhere from a minute to half an hour. It all depends on how relaxed I am, and the to-do list in my head. For me, writing is one of the ways I center in the morning. To enhance the outcome and my creative process, I anoint myself and say a gratitude prayer. Anointing with a drop of a true essential oil, I become one of the millions of people worldwide throughout seven thousand years who know this is helpful in gathering peace, focus, intention, and restoring balance. This is my typical anointing for the morning.

One drop of a blend developed for courage and confidence on my wrist pulses. My thought as I apply the drop is, I gather through the infinite source of all life, infinite love and wisdom, knowing courage to love can move mountains of fears.

As I apply another drop of another blend over my heart chakra (by the thymus gland), my thought is that I am an innocent being who loves to connect for the highest good with all of life.

Over my crown chakra (top of head directly in the middle) I use ones that open the doors between the physical world and the world of spirit. My thought is that I am fulfilling my purpose and my ability to share the love that flows through all life forms.

Why do I suggest to people that living a holistic lifestyle can improve a pet's behavior and support their well-being? My first nursing school teacher, Mrs. Norman, is my inspiration for living as toxin-free as possible. I believe that our pets, our innocent young, the wildlife, and us, benefit by using only products biologically suited to us and the planet. Mrs. Norman once asked us "what's in your toothpaste?" She explained that anything in the mouth can enter the bloodstream directly through the mucous membranes. I was hooked. Overnight, I stopped using what my family used in personal care. I've applied that philosophy to all our precious furry, feathered, finned friends who have been my roommates. As others began to ask about their pets, I offered what I have come to understand along with tuning in.

Essential oils have no regulation in the United States and some other countries. They are part of the personal care industry. Unfortunately, most companies adulterate with synthetics. Before you go out and buy any fragrance or essential oil product I would like you to know why I was asked by the director of one of the largest pharmaceutical companies to bring my reference books on essential oils along with samples to a conference room where a group of chemists would be eager to listen.

When gathered, I asked, "Why am I here?"

One chemist became the spokesperson for the group: "We all have cancer. Each one of us has a rare form, different from the other. We are the chemists for the R&D (research & development) department for fragrances. We work with synthetic fragrance development. We know it is the cause."

They were curious about the difference between synthetic and real. Essential oils are small-size molecules that are 500 AMU (atomic mass units) or smaller. That size molecule can move through the blood–brain barrier and flow into the brain. What do we want going into the brain of humans and any other beings? Essential oils are lipid soluble, they are capable of entering a cell even if the receptor sites (doors of the cells) are covered and blocked or damaged by things such as petrochemicals. When attending an international conference, one speaker, a microbiologist from Heidelberg University, Germany (Ruprecht Karl University of Heidelberg), explained how they have the capacity to enter the cells.

Essential oils fall under the FDA's warning that they cannot be used for anything except as a fragrance or food grade. I suggest if you love researching history, look up Dr. Renee Gatafosse, Dr. Jean Valnet and his books, and Dr. Daniel Penoel's *Natural Home Health Care Using Essential Oils*. Current references like the *Essential Oil Desk Reference* share a host of updated information. I have been using these precious gifts of nature's energy for supporting life, for almost two decades. Horses, injured deer, cats, dogs, fish, birds, and more have all been helped to support their natural healing abilities. Having visited aromatic plant farms in three countries along with the distilleries, I've gone through a wild learning curve. If you are concerned for yourself and your companion animals, the best simple steps are to switch to either truly unscented household and personal care products, or ones with real essential oils with a guarantee of no adulteration. Most importantly, check the ingredients of all household cleaning products for the safety of all you love. You can always email me through my website nancyorlenweber.com for any information.

As an adult, I love learning the various languages of each being I meet. The ones I have lived with, and those that I meet out and about. One sweet canine boy was a rescue. His new family had just adopted him. A local shelter told them to call me if they had concerns.

"Do we need to bring him to you? He bites and barks nonstop."

"Yes, please bring him on a leash."

In walked a fifty-pound mixed-breed while my two feline friends, Boo Girl and Kaboodle, were a few feet away, napping on the couch. They both looked up, yawned, and went back to their dreams. He stood quietly waiting with his new folks.

"Please follow me to my office."

All three were very quiet. They entered my small office, and I closed the door for privacy. The dog sauntered about with his tail wagging. He picked a spot to lay down and promptly went to sleep.

"How is that possible?" the wife asked. "He is never quiet."

"It's not magic," I said.

The scent of a space matters to every species that has an olfactory system. There are no synthetic scents in our home. No household cleaners, laundry soaps, or personal care products that can harm pets or wildlife. We have had quite a few wild furry friends enter our home. More about that later. We diffuse with essential oils to keep the air clean and free of any artificial ingredients. This boy picked up the scent even before the front door opened. His mind and body relaxed. Sometimes the love of another species can help our own lives, opening the doors of awareness to support ourselves.

Communicating with our pets always begins for me with developing a soul-to-soul connection. The practical side of that is creating a safe atmosphere. The air we share with them, the water they drink, all need to be as free of toxins as possible. During this pandemic, one of the observations many have noted is that with less pollution, many species are thriving. They are arriving in places they left long ago. They have a built-in awareness of what risks they refuse to take. Once the dangerous toxic load is gone, they come back! That's intelligence!!!

While toxins can produce odd behavior, feelings radiating from those around us and all life forms are also received, and a response can be seen. Your companion animal may not know what you are worried about; however, they will react. Some will become more protective of you; others will hide, or leave in fear. When your thoughts and feelings become upsetting to you, it's smart to take one to two minutes to quiet your mind. Three deep breaths usually help me.

While it seems simple, and maybe even what's the point of deep breathing, I find it serves well to sharpen our intuition and the ability to interpret what we get.

Look around your dwelling and find letters, note cards, and objects others have given you. Sit down with a notebook at your side. Take each item and hold it while you enter a quiet, meditative state. Observe your thoughts, feelings, and ideas. If words pop up, notice them; if images quickly flit by, note them too. Date and record all your findings. When you are ready, check out your findings. All objects—a collar, leash, food bowl, toys, a feather found—all contain energetic information. Get used to considering that being in touch with an object can relay visions, ideas, and feelings. Jot them all down. I look back over days, weeks, months, years, and decades. When first starting anything, it can feel strange, enchanting, or uncomfortable. Continuing to commit to believing there is more to discover, it becomes even more fascinating. It can also alleviate fears of the unknown. Experiencing a connection with animals, plants, and the living and deceased teaches me that the word "energy" is not just a word. The energetic fields are everywhere, communicating information in a variety of subtle ways. Learning that alleviates the fears most of us carry. Rather than be afraid of the next moment, we can live in the present of each moment, and fulfill our own spiritual purpose. That is the joy of taking a risk in looking like a fool when talking with a crow who sits on a branch watching me.

Treating every living being as if there is a divine presence operating the life force, brings the highest connection we can have. Approaching each sentient being with a consciously open heart and a flowing mind, we can notice a subtle difference in our feelings. Sometimes physical cues can occur. When I'm near a horse with a jaw issue, my jaw gets a sharp pain. Knowing it is emanating from another being, it leaves me quickly. I have been that way all my life. Being kinesthetic, I've learned to shield by firmly telling myself that it is not my energy or body that is hurting. Sometimes it is how I can help out on crime cases, including stolen animals.

Imagine your personal mind is one track, with an overlapping universal mind track that is not just connected to all else, it *is* all else. If you meditate, visualize, pray, or any method that takes you into a feeling that you are one with all, along with scents, music, and any other senses—this can support the joyful love of discovery.

In 1979, I had the privilege of meeting two wonderful women, Lynn Schroeder and Sheila Ostrander. They authored many books; one of them I read was, *Psychic Discoveries Behind the Iron Curtain*. They traveled throughout the planet. They loved research. One of the chapters introduces the Kirlians, a husband-and-wife team that showed the women their aura photography. They had just published another book, *SuperLearning* when we met. *SuperLearning 2000* is the updated version on how we learn, and the effects of certain music to keep us in both hemispheres of our brain. This helps us in our studies, whether in school or on our own. They gifted me with permission to use the techniques and create my own pieces of music.

> *Music gives a soul to the universe, wings to the mind, flight to the imagination and life to everything.* —Plato

At www.nancyorlenweber.com you can go to two blogs, "More Music/Meditation Gifts for Everyone" and "A Gift of Music for Everyone." The music was created to support being in both the right and left hemispheres of the brain. This can enhance the ability to process our intuitive faculties and our linear intelligence as companions to each other.

For scent, I have recommendations in the resources at the back of the book and on my website. There is an *Essential Oil Animal Desk Reference* and loads of social media natural help for our companion animals. Again, check the resource pages. Having gone to farms, distilleries, and taking class after class over nearly two decades on the chemistry and application of essential oils, I'm happy to suggest that if you are not aware of the potency, including the dangers of adulterating these precious gifts of the earth, research what they are capable of doing. You can always reach out to me through my website.

If you don't already send messages to trees, plants, birds, neighbors' pets, and your own furry, feathered, finned, funny friends, start now. If you see a dog coming your way, send a thought, "How old are you?" If a number pops up in your head, keep it. Ask the human how old is the dog, or say "Is your dog four?" or whatever number you felt. If the number is not close to what popped up, it may mean you are nervous or think it's impossible to know. It takes practice to trust yourself with the wireless information we download. It's an emotional journey of freeing up the highways in your universal mind, the network that is shared by all.

It was 1976 and I was invited by Andrija Puharich to his Monday night class in physics and metaphysics as his guest. If you don't know who he is, Andrija Puharich was a leader in the field of parapsychology along with a very successful inventor with about twenty patents. He introduced Uri Geller, Peter Hurkos, and Ingo Swann to the United States, all of them considered to have strong abilities as psychics.

I was introduced to him at a dinner with one of my dear friends, Dr. Edith Jurka. Edith embarked on her journey into the depths of parapsychology years before we met. I had the honor of her attendance at my classes in the mid-1970s. Edith was always eager to learn and do more. She invited me to dinner one night. Andrija arrived and sat next to me. He invited me to his Monday evening physics and metaphysics class as his guest.

The next Monday morning, I received a call from Edith.

"Marcel Vogel will be coming to Andrija's tonight. Please say hello, he is eager to talk with you."

I had no idea who this man was.

Marcel picked up the phone, and after a brief hello asked, "Can you tell me what I am holding in my hand."

I've never enjoyed being put to the test on anything. Especially when someone hasn't asked if I wanted to do this. Because I felt Edith wanted me to connect with Marcel, I took a deep breath, and shut out my dislike of the spur of the moment, drop what I'm doing, being tested.

"It's round, crystal cover, chain, and it goes tick tock."

"How did you know? It's a pocket watch!"

I left home early that evening to walk the grounds around Andrija's home. Beautiful trees graced the environment. I loved the pine tree that sat outside my home and wrote poems to and about it. As I walked that night, a lovely grandmother tree beckoned. I stood in silent communion with her. A man whom I later learned was Marcel, walked up to me saying, "Let me teach you how to communicate with that tree."

A friend who was with me responded with, "That's like teaching a fish how to swim."

Marcel walked away. When we gathered in Andrija's living room for class, Marcel was invited to teach. He took a potted plant and placed it in the center of the room. He then guided us into a meditative state. We were instructed to place our hands near the plant and imagine our energy traveling through our fingers into the roots of the plant. As we continued this exercise, exploring the stem and the flower, it was easy to set aside the part of the mind that says this is silly. After the meditation we all shared our experience. It was interesting to observe that most of us felt the plant distinctly unhappy with its windowsill home. It wanted to move to another part of the room. Andrija happily complied, and took the plant to where we believed it would be comfortable. Several weeks later it was apparent that we heard the plant. It had never produced blossoms before. It became beautifully vibrant with colorful flowers. If you have a plant, any plant, why not take a break from reading? Go talk with your plant!

Marcel later gifted me with a photo of a liquid crystal. I had no idea who Marcel was, just another person interested in the same things Andrija, Edith, and a bunch of us were. All of us fascinated by our connection with all of life. It's only recently that I have learned of his many accomplishments.

He received 32 patents for his inventions up through his tenure at IBM. Among these was the magnetic coating for the 24-inch hard disk drive systems. His areas of expertise, besides luminescence, were phosphor technology, magnetics, and liquid crystal systems. His own company developed luminescence for black light, fluorescent crayons, and more.

Marcel was featured in the first episode of "In Search Of" hosted by Leonard Nimoy, called "Other Voices." He gave his theories regarding the possibility of communication between plants.

From marcelvogel.org there is a chart that the following refers to:

Marcel said that squiggle on the script chart recorder changed his life. This was the beginning of Marcel's transformation from being a purely rational scientist to becoming a mystical scientist. It was found that plants respond to the thought of being cut, burned, or torn. He discovered that if he tore a leaf from one plant, a second plant would respond, but only if he was paying attention to it.

The plants seemed to be mirroring his own mental responses. He concluded that the plants were acting like batteries, storing the energy of his thoughts and intentions.

He said of these experiments: "I learned that there is energy connected with thought. Thought can be pulsed, and the energy connected with it becomes coherent and has a laser-like power."

One of the most exciting books out is a best seller. Author Peter Wohlleben convincingly makes the case that trees are social beings.

We all need to let go of the need to figure out what we are experiencing until after our experience. We tend to intellectualize to avoid the next moment. It's your turn to play. If you have plants, it might be fun for you to start working with them as living beings. They love company. For further ideas on the plant kingdom, read "The Man Who Talked to Plants: The Visionary Research of Cleve Backster" at http://www.consciouslifestylemag.com/cleve-backster-research-plants/. Quoting one part: "A new study published recently in the scientific journal *Biomed Central Ecology* may have finally tipped the scale in Backster and Bose's favor. The research demonstrates evidence that plants can indeed communicate with each other, and they do so by using nano-mechanical sound waves." Plants communicate, and so do all life forms; we simply need to start with that knowledge, and work towards increasing our ability to be available to listen and learn.

Each species has its own language, yet some are closer to our ways than others. I decided it was easiest for me to simply treat every life form as an individual created through love. That has led to some interesting moments. One of those moments I was with a client as I opened the door for her to leave. A black bear was about fifteen feet from me walking up our brick ramp, probably to come to the door. I told my client to stay inside.

Staring at the bear I spoke and sent messages of adoring her (I hoped she was a she): "Mama, I know you love the woods. While you may be looking for food, I'd suggest you go up into the woods. Leave the children next door alone."

She turned to go away, and started down toward the street. We live about seventy feet up from the street.

"I said not to go down to where the children are," I stated firmly.

I started to walk towards her. Now all I felt was that she knew better. Like someone willful, she was debating whether to continue or head to the woods. She turned her head to look at me. I stared back with a laser-focused thought, go back into the woods now. I was talking to her as if she was a recalcitrant being who knew better and was just stubborn. I was just as stubborn. She bowed her head and went upwards into the woods. A month later the black bear came back to show off her three adorable cubs.

Animals can communicate quite well. And they do. And generally speaking, they are ignored. —Alice Walker

We don't need to know sonar, clicks, or bird songs to communicate, yet when we attempt to reach out, they all know. Treat your own being as if you have a phenomenal translating machine. Take the risk and assume you heard the other being and respond. Sometimes that is all takes.

CHAPTER 2

Cats are my Teachers

While it is common for us to believe we can communicate with our companions, whether furry, feathered, scaly, finned or from the insect kingdom, it takes a bit of a leap to know all life communicates.

I began to put the pieces together when I worked at my last nursing job as Head Nurse of the Acute Psychiatric Unit in the old Lincoln Hospital in the Bronx. It has since been torn down, and a new one built in its place. It still remains very much alive in my mind and heart. It is where I could see that using these precious gifts of encouraging my soul to be my guide, had a strong purpose. More on that in my next book.

When a physical disability and some incidents (next book) made it difficult to continue to work as a nurse, I resigned. Staying home in a two-bedroom, one-bathroom converted barn, I began to practice deep breathing to keep my spinal injuries and defects from running my life. As I practiced, I began synthesizing the world within.

One day my neighbor on Wooddale Avenue in Peekskill, called asking if I saw her cat. An image and a thought popped up together.

Without hesitation I said, "Your cat is playing in a swamp. He will be home tomorrow at 3:00 p.m. tomorrow."

"How do you know? You saw him?"

"No, I don't even know if there is a swamp. I am sharing what popped up for me."

"You're crazy."

Obviously to her I was now a crazed woman living near a sane one. Until 3:00 p.m. the next day, when her muddy cat showed up at her door. She called to let me know. Now I became the neighbor with some weird abilities. The universe was sending me a test to see if what others thought of me was as important as the gifts given to me. I passed, for the moment. It no longer bothered me that others didn't get it, that others backed away frightened. One of the gifts of working with the Albert Einstein hospital complex at Lincoln Hospital, were the doctors taking their residency training in psychiatry. One of them, Dr. Peter Kimmel, introduced me to the work of Dr. Thomas Szasz. I read his book, *Manufacture of Madness: A Comparative Study of the Inquisition and the Mental Health Movement*.

The short version is that it showed a clear indictment of the resentment by licensed physicians fearing loss of work to the women of the villages who created ointments, salves, talked, listened, prayed with their neighbors, and used any of their gifts to be of service. They were trusted by all. When labeling them witches no longer worked, they were then called insane and thrown into insane asylums. Up until the 1930s, in the United States and elsewhere there were insane asylums. History helps me understand that despite many who feared or fear what many of us think of as gifts, it has always been a problem for those who hold shame, guilt, and/ or secrets.

The work itself on the psych unit was the best teamwork I had ever participated in; from the orderly to the Chief of Psychiatry, we all pitched in to assist some very dysfunctional people that came to our unit. We definitely were into creating magic, and we succeeded again and again. It is why I began to treat these odd occurrences of knowing beyond our usual senses, as the gifts they are. When I left my nursing career it was time to discover a new path. My feline and canine buddies were great teachers, as they brought me new lessons.

Mu, an exquisite, long-haired, male feline was one of my gurus. I don't know if he was an atheist, pagan, or God-centered being, but all his actions demonstrated that he lived within a code of ethics filled with integrity, compassion, kindness, humor, and love.

It was 1974 and Sweetie Pi R squared and I were best buds. She slept on my pillow with me, and still played *I can scratch your hand faster than you can pull it away* into her later years. When Sweetie Pi was pregnant she came to me with a problem. In my mind I heard, *Mommy, I have problems with the babies inside me.*

I believed what I thought transpired, and took her to our vet. We were good friends with the vet and his wife. I rushed in and he examined her, saying he couldn't detect any problems. Days later I awakened with her on a blanket with two dead babies by her side. I swear she was crying. It was six in the morning when I called our vet at his home. He came over in his pj's, stethoscope in hand.

"She has one more inside of her. Let's wait until noon. If nothing happens then, I will give her Pitocin to stimulate contractions."

"She said don't wait. Nothing will move and Pitocin won't work."

Noon came, we rushed to his hospital. She was given Pitocin. Nothing happened. The vet's wife and I were present when he operated and brought out her kitten, not breathing. His wife took the little guy, turned him upside down and gently kept stroking his body until he started to breathe. We named him Michael, after the vet. He was a beautiful black, long-haired guy.

Michael had been a difficult child for Sweetie Pi. Born after the C-section, she, like her mother, held him in her arms and cried. She shed more tears in her life then some men I've known. When it came time to weaning him, she would not hear of it, and stalked away yelling at all of us. She would lick off whatever substance we placed on her nipples so that her son could continue nursing, until she decided when he was six months old, that it was time. The Veterinarian kept insisting she would develop problems, but the only problem she developed was Michael's lack of hunting instincts. One day, she grabbed a mouse and put it in the water bowl. She stalked across the slate kitchen floor and talked to Michael. We sat at our woven cane kitchen chairs watching her direct him to the mouse. Michael went over and took the mouse out of the bowl, gave her or him a few licks, and proudly smiled at mama as if to say, *Aren't you proud of me, I saved a mouse's life!* To Michael's surprise, mama would not play with him the rest of the day.

A few days later, Sweetie Pi tried again, this time out on our hilly lawn. The grass was tall enough for her to pretend her white with black markings could be camouflaged. No one argued with her. She could catch anything, except when Michael stalked her. He was not quiet. He tromped after her, jumping with ecstasy at the new game. He destroyed any possibility of follow through with the loudest meows. Sweetie Pi literally threw up her paws in frustration, and never tried to teach him again.

Michael was eleven months old when he was killed by a dog (not ours). His burial was attended by his family. Sweetie Pi stayed by my side in shock. In the ancient tradition, we took artifacts that we believed were special. Rebecca (my daughter) gave him a favorite toy to take on his new journey; Jesse (my son) also gave him one of his toys; I gave him flowers; and Sweetie Pi cried.

A little over one year slid by and there was a storm rattling our windows. I went to look outside, and there was an all-white long-haired feline rolling around at our doorstep. This became a daily occurrence. He would not enter our home for the first few weeks, yet he would eat as if he were starved. The odd part is, we discovered he lived a few streets down, seemed happy there, and just took off to our home. He decided to let us adopt him. The family who lived with him concurred, it seemed the only thing to do. He was eleven months old when he decided to be ours.

I didn't think anything of this, being a little slow sometimes. I was amazed when Sweetie Pi had absolutely no animosity. This was the Queen who swatted both cats and dogs alike when they first arrived, ensuring they knew she was in charge. He arrived and she said, *Yes, Yes, Yes.* From the moment they met, they were inseparable, except when she went to hunt. He followed her everywhere at first, and then they reached a compromise. He would stay inside when she hunted.

The reason was obvious: birds loved him, mice loved him, dogs loved him. He had no enemies, and he loved them all. We named him Mu, for Lemuria in honor of the wisdom of the ages that poured through him as naturally as water down a fall. He was Michael all over again.

Mu liked to lie outside in the early morning and be among the mourning doves as they ate on our porch. They always accepted his presence and just walked around him. Once in a while, another species of bird would dance up above his head and he would just sit there being entranced by its beauty. These were the times Sweetie Pi was not permitted outdoors. The birds would never come if she was out.

One sunny spring day, in the mid-1970s, a neighbor called asking if her mom could stop by.

"My mother is a member of the Audubon Society. Every time she passes your home she sees birds that she hasn't seen in Westchester County (New York) in years."

Her mom dropped in. Flowery dress, sweet voice, and gray hair accompanied this happily anxious woman as she opened my screen door. She sat facing the outside like a true bird watcher. We spoke while she kept her eyes on the air right above our porch.

"Look, a Titmouse," she said with delight.

I kept looking for a mouse with you know what. So much for my species identification abilities.

"That's the very pretty gray bird to the right," she said.

She was used to explaining to children like me. Mu stood in front of me, then walked to the screen door. I got his message and opened it for him. A few seconds passed and he was ready to come in again. In his mouth was the titmouse, gently held with its eyes open and peaceful. Mu went and stood in front of the woman, who promptly screamed.

"Mu, she doesn't understand. You'll have to let him go back outside."

I opened the screen door again and Mu walked, head held high, onto the porch.

"Please stop screaming; he just wanted to help."

She stopped, all right. Mouth opened wide, she watched the titmouse fly within inches of Mu's head for a few minutes, and then land on his head proudly while Mu took his *I am a sleepy cat* position, fully stretched. I could swear he and the Titmouse were laughing at the absurdity of someone being frightened for one of two best friends. Again my neighbors talked.

Mu enjoyed a good rescue. Being the responsible, evolved soul, he felt it was his duty to help wherever he could. I came to rely on Mu's common sense when we adopted Creamsicle, who was a male feline, abandoned like so many others. From the beginning, he seemed a bit strange. Although he was less than three months old when we adopted him, he began to wander off immediately. Mu would know where he was, and when I called out for Creamsicle, Mu would search and rescue.

Marianne was our babysitter. At fifteen, she was the eldest of five children. She would, when the need arose, feed our feline friends. So when we were going on an overnight trip, Marianne stopped by for instructions.

"Marianne, if Creamsicle gets outside and you can't find him, go to Mu and tell him to get Creamsicle."

"Uh-huh."

"Marianne, you don't have to believe me, just do it."

"I promise."

The next day all seemed quiet when I got back; Creamsicle and Mu were asleep together on the living room sofa. Marianne stopped by in the evening after her basketball practice.

"My family can't stop talking about Mu," she said. "Yesterday as I opened the door to get in, Creamsicle dashed out and up a tree. I turned to Mu and said, 'Mu, Creamsicle ran up a tree, please get him.' I didn't raise my voice. It was just like a conversation with a friend. Mu ran out of the house, and dashed over to the tree where Creamsicle was residing. Mu climbed the tree, and I swear he was yelling at Creamsicle. When he got to Creamsicle, he jumped over him and bumped him downward. He kept doing this, until he got him down to the ground, and then continued to yell at him as he poked and pushed him into the house! How could he know?"

And so Marianne opened her mind's heart to more wondrous possibilities. Hopefully, that experience has enriched her life. It certainly has mine. Mu brought so many treasured moments to my heart. My prayerful wish is that his soul is continuing its grand adventure somewhere, somehow, in the divine light of creation.

Then we moved to Budd Lake, New Jersey in 1979. Down the hill from us was a busy road, Route 46. Sitting with Mu and Sweetie Pi, I mentally drew picture after picture of the road with speeding cars, and warned them with a mix of pictures and emotions what could happen. Shooting this along the psychic highway from my heart and mind, Mu and Sweetie Pi acknowledged the heart talk by sending me back oceans of adoring, affectionate, mommy thoughts. My whole being felt satisfied with a deep inner sense of well-being. They understood never to go to the highway. That same afternoon an older couple (probably younger than I am now), called us to come get our cat. Their house was at the corner of Route 46 and our street, Wildwood Ave. Alongside their cottage were several acres of woods that led all the way up to our lawn. They saw the new, all-white longhaired cat head into their woods. They asked if someone could come get him. Rebecca was selected to bring Mu back home. The next day, another call from the couple. Again, Rebecca went out and retrieved Mu. The next day when the couple called, I went. We met outside their door.

"We have thirty cats and we never let them out," the woman of the couple said. "They could get killed."

"Mu is not suicidal. He's just checking out his new surroundings."

"You really shouldn't let him out. Now we'll never get him back. He went into the woods. We couldn't hold on to him."

"Don't worry, if it happens again, as I'm sure it will, just talk to him. He listens. Look, I'll show you. Mu, mommy's here, please come out, sweetheart."

Mu scampered out of the woods, rubbed my legs, and looked up at me.

"Mu, my love, these people are afraid you'll get hurt; they don't understand. Please go home and I'll try to help them understand. OK?"

The poor couple just kept watching as Mu trotted back up the hill, obediently seeking our door where the children were waiting.

"See? All you need to do next time, is call him and tell him to go home. If he doesn't listen to you, just call me and I'll send him a thought."

The next day our local newspaper had a photo on the cover of Mu, Sweetie Pi, our dog Ramona, Rebecca, Jesse, and me. It was about the work I had done recovering missing animals. The headline was *Psychic Communicates with Animals.* I always wondered what the couple must have thought when they picked up the paper. They never called again. *Guru Mu* taught me to stretch beyond my beliefs and seek common ground with all animals.

**From left to right: Jesse, Nancy, Ramona, Rebecca and Sweetie Pi
(the math Pi, not the food!)**

*If having a soul means being able to feel love and loyalty and
gratitude, then animals are better off than a lot of humans.*
—James Herriot

The best homework I found is creating the belief and learning to live
within it. Some of the fabulous books that have inspired and encouraged so
many of us to do our work are: *Kinship with All Life,* by J. Allen Boone (yes,
a relative of Daniel Boone), *and The Parrot's Lament,* by Eugene Linden.
Author and retired animal communicator, Penelope Smith has a great website with lots of helpful information to encourage your journey.

Domesticated animals in today's world, particularly ones like dogs
and cats, have stronger olfactory systems than we do. They can have a

tougher time with the toxic chemical cleaners in our homes. I had just anointed my crown chakra with a woodsy blend, and walked down our driveway to get the day's mail. Cosmos, a yellow lab, was being walked on a leash. They were passing me by when tail wagging, jumping for joy, he tried to stay and play with me.

"That's weird," said the woman walking Cosmos. "He has never gone to another person, only me."

"It's not just me, it is a scent I wear that reminds him of things he loves."

She left without another word. Yes, I must seem strange to some. It's a good thing I've learned that strange just means I decide for myself who I am.

Whether your pet is alive or deceased, start recording your conversations. It helps to keep notes, dates of occurrences and details, even drawings of visions. It can take time to sort out how we perceive another and more time to interpret, accept, and enjoy an ongoing flow of shared thoughts.

If the animal is deceased, use either a photo or an item you kept that was his or hers. If you believe that our frequency matters, then apply essential oils to assist in centering to harmonize with your highest frequency. A bit anxious that it won't happen? Music that is bilateral, hemi-synch, or simply calming for you will also help. Mentally ask to be available for the highest good for both of you. Believe the two of you are meeting and go from there. Imagination is the ladder to the soul, and the soul is what can meet all others here, and on the other side. Once you feel you are restless, close the conversation, and write down what occurred. When at least a month has passed, read what you wrote from the beginning of recording your findings. I've looked back again and again over the years. It has taught me that all life is my kin. We humans wrap ourselves in a fabric of belief and disbelief, acceptance and argument, and intellectual debates about existence while Baby, a most precious groundhog, lived in the moment. We called her Brahma (Great Soul) Baby.

My love of groundhogs developed through the friendship of a family of three groundhogs with a feline named Boo Girl. In 1981, Boo Girl's mommy had abandoned her seven children on the grounds of a local institution, after a fumigator commenced war on their home. Fortunately, the fumigator saw the babies, and called the local animal warden. Seven stranded kittens waited for help.

My girlfriend Sue had a shelter where I had already obtained our dog, Ramona. That summer, Sue needed a break and had taken me up on my offer to help, "Anything you need, just call." If you say those words, remember there is an occasional person who will believe you. Sue asked me to take in all the rescued kittens for the summer. Twenty-one kittens graced us with their presence that summer.

Seven wild kittens were brought to our home in a cage hissing along with the tiniest set of claws and teeth. We put their cage in the "red room." At the time I lived in Budd Lake, New Jersey in a large stone house. The "red room" was a 25-by-25-foot living room that adjoined another 25-by-25-foot living room through French doors. All this second living room contained were white walls and a red carpet. It's the room in which my children loved practicing gymnastics, bringing wizards' spells forward with a slashing wooden wand, and dancing. Although we have since moved, and others have now probably done away with the beautiful emptiness of the space, I still see it as the room that always waited. So the cage found a home, at least until all seven babies felt safe enough to come out and play.

The first one out of the cage spoke lamb—the sweetest, gentle baa-baa sound broke through that furball. She remained a lamb speaker; no meow was ever heard throughout her 19 years of life. Her wavy short brown and beige fur reminded me of a bobcat. My two children decided to name her Boo Girl, since if we made the slightest move she ran. She would always hide when other folks were around. The other six were taught to trust humans through the love, patience, and compassion, of Rebecca and Jesse. They would lie perfectly still for hours at a time, in the same room with the terrified kittens. After almost three weeks, all but one would happily climb the people mountains and play. As they became accustomed to playing on the backs of two still children, hands would gently reach out to stroke them. By the end of the third week, all were relating to humans well, and Rebecca and Jesse could move around enjoying the abundant delight that was now present in our little friends. We unanimously agreed that while Boo Girl was the friendliest towards us, she was also the most terrified. She would cuddle and then bolt at the slightest movement. If I called out, "Boo Girl, it's only mommy," she would pitifully baa-baa her way back to one of our waiting arms.

Next kitten out was Maxine. She escaped into the woods. For three months she stayed there. We left food outside, bringing it closer and closer to home, hoping to lure her back. Jesse, age 6 at the time, was the hero. He would stand outside calling her to him. One bright summer day, it happened. She placed her long calico fur under the palms of his hands and purred. She was back with us.

Now they were ready for new homes. Boo Girl's siblings were easily given loving homes through the shelter's adoption screening program. Boo Girl took to our tiniest family member, a silver-tipped tabby, Tina. She was our yogi master. Until Tina's death, she could do yoga postures, including lying on her back in your arms with complete devotion to whomever she was with. Beauty, a rescued mourning dove, loved flying onto Tina's back and perching for a picture. Boo Girl, like everyone else, loved Tina. Tina loved everyone, and would happily bring Boo Girl on her side of the bed, far away from the evil eye of Amy. Amy, our largest feline resident, believed that she set the rules. And within her claw reach, she did. She loved people of all ages, especially children. They could scrunch her up and she would purr louder. Her claws were reserved for felines, all except Tina. To all who met her, Tina shared her heart and soul and they in turn opened their hearts to her.

**Four month old Tina on Jesse's head
and four month old Boo Girl in his arms.**

Boo Girl quickly decided that both indoors and outdoors had opportunities for pleasure. She began hanging out by a boulder. Okay, it was a large rock, but I couldn't budge it. If you opened our front door, walked ten feet across and about six feet down the hill towards the street, you would come to this oversized rock that would need blasting to be moved. This was a most intriguing place for her. One day, I looked out and saw Boo Girl sleeping with three groundhogs on the boulder. It was impossible to disguise her; there she was, the miniature-looking bobcat, warm browns, splashes of burnt orange and black, with fur soft as a lamb. It went well with her sounds. Neighbors teased me when recounting this spectacular sight.

"Groundhogs? Are you sure? Maybe you need glasses."

Several weeks later, two neighbors joined me in a hunt for great clothes at end-of-the-season sales. To return and enter my driveway we had to pass the front yard. Four groundhogs were dancing playfully. The car sounds disturbed their musical ears and they disbanded, all running in separate directions, three towards the woods and one silly feline towards our door. You should have heard the talk in my neighborhood.

Boo Girl continued to enjoy many good years of friendship with the groundhog family until we moved to another town. Anytime I moved to an area that could prove dangerous or upsetting to our animal friends, I would sit down and send them images along with emotionally charged thoughts of the forthcoming changes. This is as important as telling my children we are moving. Every being needs to adjust to changes that are beyond their control. Divorced, house sold, we moved locally to Flanders, New Jersey, another part of the same town. That way the children could still attend the same schools. Boo Girl seemed to understand and took to walking around the cul de sac of this new area late at night, the shy thing that she was.

Around that time Janice Hall, a friend and astrologer, wanted a reading. After her reading, she brought out my natal chart and offered to reciprocate.

"You will be with your soulmate in two years. He's a Capricorn, music will have something to do with your meeting, and he will bring organization to your world like you have never seen. You will love him completely and forever."

I was not pleased. Disinterested was the only word I could think of to describe a permanent relationship. I was now happily strong, independent, and very content being single. I left hoping she was wrong. Turns out she was right, and Boo Girl benefitted from the relationship. It started with music. I had collaborated with a friend, Elaine Silver, in writing twelve songs. Elaine is a gifted folk singer-composer, about whom Tom Chapin had glibly remarked, "I'm her closing act." Two of our songs became some of Elaine's performance favorites. You can hear them at <u>nancyorlenweber.</u> <u>com</u>. I am always humbled and delighted to hear Elaine sing my words. Mesmerized by the experience, I became something of a groupie. When she said that she was opening for Loudon Wainwright at the Stanhope House in Stanhope, New Jersey, I took advantage of another opportunity to hear our songs.

Another friend of Elaine's, Dick Weber, was also in the audience. He introduced himself and I immediately took to disliking him. We then met again as volunteers for the environmental movement. Dr. Wally Burnstein was a friend who was looking to stop food irradiation plants. He had successfully sued one such manufacturer who had a major leak. It was across the street from a school. The court found the company guilty and they had to pay two-and-a-half-million dollars for the cleanup. That was in the 1980s. Turns out we had both been friends with Wally separately because we were eager to help, and be part of the solution.

Two years later, Dick joined a nonprofit that I started with my dear friend, Sue Velicoff Pelechaty. Thinking and swearing that I would neither fall in love again nor marry again, I landed in Dick's arms and have stayed there ever since. Oh yes, organizing. He is the least organized person I know; consequently, I have become immersed in organizing everything I possibly can!

When Dick and I married, my feline buddies, Boo Girl, Tina, Amy, and Sweetie Pi, along with my son, Jesse, and I, moved to Dick's ranch-style home in a lake community. With lots of wildlife and acres of woods, it is the perfect place for all of us. Boo Girl promptly took to sitting for hours outside on a stone wall waiting for what she hoped was her new friend, Brahma Baby.

Baby, a beautiful groundhog, had been born that year and her mom left ASAP. Baby was as disinterested in a relationship with Boo Girl as I had been when I first met Dick. She would not even look at Boo Girl. We have a stone wall about four-and-a-half feet high, where our leftover food is left for the deer, squirrels, and whoever else wanders by. Baby liked melon, cantaloupe in particular. I began leaving a bigger piece for Baby. Boo Girl would drool, not for melon, not for food, but for friendship.

After weeks of Baby eating on the ledge of the wall, I felt a change in our relationship. Following my heart right out the back door, I stopped beside Baby. My right hand reached out and stroked her beautiful back, while she continued her melon binge. Her head turned, eyes directly on me, a moment of acknowledgment, and then she simply continued to eat. Baby finished her dinner and turned back up the hill to her sleeping quarters. Boo Girl had been watching by our sliding glass door. Later that night I had a class in my living room. The attendees knew my family for a few years.

"When did you get this precious cat?" Linda asked, as she petted Boo Girl. No one except the immediate family had ever seen Boo Girl until that night.

"Twelve years ago."

Boo Girl proceeded to introduce herself to each and every visitor, cuddling sweetly in their arms. She remained friendly to all visitors who entered our home until she was nineteen, when she laid in my arms, and gently left this earth for her next adventure. I know she is with Brahma Baby and all her friends from Budd Lake.

Then there are the moments where a cat teaches me science. I was sitting in a living room with a woman who asked me to find out why one of her three cats had been peeing in the kitchen for a while. I sent messages of love to the cats. One suddenly sent a message back of fear. Curious, I sent back, *Who or what are you afraid of?* The cat's mind showed a huge lion lurking in the kitchen. How could that be? By asking myself, I took whatever popped up next. Three months was the only other thought that I received. Suddenly it came together like the last piece of a puzzle.

I turned to the woman and said "Did you change cleaning products for the kitchen three months ago?"

"Yes."

"And your ginger-colored cat started peeing after that?"

"Yes!"

"Did you switch to ammonia?"

"Yes, how do you know that?"

"Because ammonia smells like cat pee. And that cat believes it is a huge lion peeing. Stop using ammonia."

It was done. She switched products, and the cat was no longer scared of the lion. Sometimes it is that simple, and other times we need a little more help. The next year I was called in to another home by a couple who had taken in three cats, each at a different time. Because they appeared to hate each other, they were relegated to the unfinished basement. Each cat took a corner to hide in. A bowl of food and water by their corners, and a few feet away, their own litter box. The couple were seeking last-ditch help before giving them all away.

By my request we three sat in the middle of the basement. I put on music that I use for humans, plants, mammals, and birds. Music with guided imagery is there for you to use for yourself and all companion life forms. Music turned on, I then took a blend of essential oils that support stress management and applied five drops onto an unbleached coffee filter. I put it on the floor by my feet. I turned on the music from my blog.

We talked about the cats while each of them had slowly come out of hiding. They began making their way to where we were. Twenty minutes later they were all curled up together by my feet. Toxins used for cleaning can change behavior; so can fear. When everyone was peaceful, the cats felt at home, finally. That was the beginning of a sweeter time for the whole family.

"Music is the language of the spirit. It opens the secret of life bringing peace, abolishing strife." —Kahlil Gibran

Entering into the situation without preconceived notions, and mentally affirming it is for the highest good for all, sets the intention to be harmless. The truth has no limits. Talk with wildlife, talk with companion animals, fish, birds, plants, and so on. If there are none near you, ask friends to send you photographs online, or mail, and talk as if the animal in the photo is with you. Keep notes, preferably in a journal, and date them, along with all details.

CHAPTER 3

Birds are my Teachers

When my daughter's fourth-grade class had a spring break, we offered to take home the pair of lovebirds that lived at the Montessori school she attended. We decided to put their cage in the living room.

Every Thursday night our living room would become the classroom for adults interested in meditation, creative visualization, healing, and psychic development. Two Thursday nights passed before the birds were brought back to the Montessori school. There was an egg in the cage when we returned them. The teacher, who had raised these and other lovebirds, was surprised. They had never laid eggs before. We all came to believe it was the loving peace that my students entered into, that gave the lovebirds the atmosphere they sought.

Find the time daily to release the stress, let go of fear, and connect to the divine. It's been done forever because it works. Devote yourself to your own peace. Watch the world around you enjoy the flow of light and love that emanates from your presence.

Letting the intuition and intellect blend well, takes practice. During the few minutes when you are observing without judgement, you might receive some information or feelings. It will be clear they are not your usual thoughts or feelings. If you can carefully assess your thoughts, feelings, images, ideas, and words that pop up, and anything else that occurred, you're on your way to that wonderful world that St. Francis of Assisi entered during his awakening.

Scottie, our precious grand-daughter, was seven. We were taking her to a zoo in Richmond, Virginia, on one of our visits. Scottie and I had a running argument. She thought I was silly believing that animals talk. I thought she needed help to understand what I meant. We had just finished petting a giraffe when she spotted a peacock. He was at the far end of the very large cage.

"Oh, I've never seen them with their feathers open," she said.

That was enough for grandma. I got her to agree to "send love" with me to the peacock. I followed my usual protocol inwardly saying "my soul greets your soul, you are a beautiful soul, and I hope our company helps you cope with the home you are now living in. Would you be so kind as to demonstrate the beauty of your feathers?" Most importantly, I could feel the love flowing to this beloved soul. Now, we had been in this small zoo for over an hour. Although Scottie had not noticed him before, I had. He had remained in the corner all the time.

Almost as soon as the message left my heart, the peacock turned around, walked over towards us, and graced us with his plumage fanned out as wide as he could. He repeated this several times. I could feel his being, waiting to know if this was good. I kept sending him back messages of marvel at the wonder of his beauty. He then gracefully turned and walked back to his contemplating corner. One peacock made a believer out of one little girl. I promised that peacock I would always love him.

Talk to a lot of different animals. Stand in their presence as if you are greeting Creation—for of course, you are. Mind to mind, heart to heart, send blessings and gratitude for the meeting. Notice each response. Some will be very aware and respond immediately; others will not pay you the slightest attention. Some will play shy for a while, and others will display fear or anger. Each being responds to the Light from his or her own state of being. Do not take anything personal, not even success. The more you practice, the quicker the centering, the easier the signals go out through you to whomever and whatever you are focused upon. Be very careful at this stage. Focused power is leashed by ethics. Never send anger or fear. Keep them to yourself. It is reasonable to experience an array of emotions, but it is not reasonable to wield them as a power against others or back on yourself. Fear can harm yourself.

My first nursing instructor, Mrs. Norman, told me, "Place your negative emotions in a bag when you are entering into your work. Pick them up afterwards, if you still want them."

I have been using her statement ever since. Love for life has a rippling effect. Standing in the light of love, the reflection we receive is of more love. Do you remember any time when you had someone help you build the trust of your own powers to love both yourself and others? If so, doesn't that help you through difficult circumstances? Then let's believe that the plant, the dog, the crow, and more also benefit by our sharing soul to soul, heart to heart.

A popular helpful slogan about troubles in the world is "When you see something, say something." What about seeing on TV or reading about a devastating hurricane where pets are stranded, a puppy lost, or beached whales? Know in your heart that you can be of service. At that moment, you can convert a helpless feeling to a feeling of love of service. Imagine you are a wise and great healer, filled with gentle yet strong love emanating from your soul. Your soul has now opened to receive a different frequency of energy, a universal flow that can run through you, not from you. Your personal energy is protected from being drained. Centered on the belief that the self has a unique frequency apart from the flow that is shared with all is a natural shield. The moment you believe that, you are there. Whether you mentally send waves of love, have a kind and supportive thought that is being sent, or converse with the being you are holding in the light, you are now making a difference.

Every day, practice placing a greeting in your mind and heart, and send it. Image your friend receiving your blanket of love. Trust your intuition. Remember simple truths: if it is harmless to you and others, do it. There was a man in our county, Len Soucy, renowned as one of the leading experts on raptor surgery. He had taught many veterinarians how to perform specific surgeries on raptors. He never went to vet school; he never took training. He simply opened his heart to a raptor in trouble years ago, and did what his spirit compelled him to. He did not argue with his inner voice, he did not argue with his circumstances, he did not consciously seek to become an expert with raptors. His soul took him there. He complied. At https://theraptortrust.org/2017/10/nj-raptor-refuge-continues-legacy-of-compassion/ you can read how love sparked a great rippling effect that has helped people who see a bird in trouble have a place to take it to heal.

Speaking of rescue birds, it was a warm evening, 6:40 p.m. to be exact, and the couple my husband and I were talking with was contemplating their wedding. This was the first time we met with them. Dick and I each perform wedding ceremonies. When we can, we like to sit in on each other's interviews. Hearing couple's stories of their first meeting, when they fell in love, funny proposals, and all the wrappings of relationship happiness, delights both of us. We have met fabulous people from all walks of life this way. That night was a double treat.

Shari and Sean were delightful to talk with. They were saying something, when I noticed out of the corner of my eye a flash of something dropping out of a pine tree on our lawn. Dick saw it at the same time, and left the porch to walk over to the tree. I saw him bend down and scoop something. His mutterings were beyond comprehension. It sounded like he was upset. Holding out his hand to me, I took the tiniest bird I had ever seen. It was somewhere between one and three days old, and as we later discovered, a mourning dove. Thank you Mu, our dear cat who loved birds. You sent us a Beauty.

Dick's comment: "It's a baby bird and it will probably die."

"Not if we can help it! Hurry, while I hold her, you go to the pet store, and get her some food."

Dick drove to the pet store, getting there just as it was closing (a very good omen), and returned with baby bird mush, bird syringes and instructions.

"I asked the staff at the store what to do, and a woman shopping said she rescued birds and handed me the product of baby mush food."

Feeding Beauty was interesting, I tried. Like most mothers, I was awed by her appearance. Feeding her was another matter. Every fifteen minutes, around the clock, she had to be fed. This mommy couldn't do it. I fell asleep with her in my hands, and prayed that she would survive the night. Mentally covering her with prayer, light, love, and anything else the universe could provide, I awakened to a starving child. Did you ever try to feed a mourning dove? They don't open their mouths like other birds. In fact, they keep it shut and toss their head side to side to spit out the food. That was day five or six. That's when I knew she would survive. Just like some of us, when we start recovering our strength, we get ornery.

After several days of battle with our stubborn infant, Dick and I were sure that this little bird did not fall from the nest, she was pushed. How did a mother mourning dove feed her babies? As we later learned, doves are raised on "crop milk," which the parents force down chicks' throats. Our lack of awareness was another very fortuitous circumstance for our new Beauty. She would spit, and we would gently push it back in again and again.

Beauty slept in a basket, and then on our dresser. She stayed in my hair during the day or on my shoulder. I tried to teach her to coo, but she still ignored my attempts. Dick taught her to fly, running with her on his arm and then gently flinging her in the air. She took to eating on our living room floor, kitchen table, and porch. Tina, our silver-tipped tabby cat, fell in love with Beauty. Beauty reciprocated by sitting on Tina's back and letting her be the protector when out on the porch. Our other feline friends didn't care either way. Boo Girl wasn't interested in anyone except Baby, the groundhog, and Amy, our fourteen-pound feline, wasn't getting up for anything less than a hug or food.

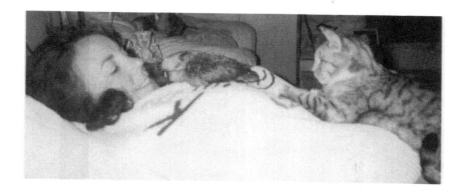

Nap Time for Nancy, Beauty and Tina

Our neighbor called out one day, "Is that your bird who visits us?"

"I don't know, what does it look like?"

"It's brownish grey and small with a young face. I opened our door yesterday and the thing just walked right in past our four cats, into the kitchen and up on the table, where it proceeded to eat the leftover cereal."

"That's our Beauty. Isn't she wonderful!"

Mama and Dad were so proud of her. We still rejoice in the image. A few weeks later, Beauty was flying, albeit crooked. She would stay out for a few hours, then strut back in past the open door, jump up onto my shoulder and busy herself watching the world. One night, while teaching meditation in my living room, all heads turned in unison. Beauty was staring in, perched on a rope that was lying above our outdoor wooden swing. I opened the door and she flew in, landing on the telephone by one of the students. We took it to mean an important call would be coming for this student. Then she flew across the room onto my shoulder where she remained peacefully joined with us in meditation.

Beauty and Nancy gardening

That was Beauty's last night with us. She slept on our dresser, leaving a string of "pearls," and the next morning played outside watching Mama in the garden. In the midst of my weeding, Beauty flew onto my head. I felt her bid me goodbye as she flew across the garden, across the road and into a very old, very high tree far beyond my reach. Another child was leaving home. It reminded me of when my son went off to college. We drove him up to Amherst, parked his stuff, had a happy time with him, and all the way home I played harmonica and sang, knowing he was going to fly a little at a time.

Beauty's leaving was different. I didn't feel as safe. My fear level was high and I couldn't sort out what it indicated. Learning to differentiate between fact and fiction, imagination and psychic perception, is a continuous process. The next day a storm erupted, one of those tearing storms that pulls telephone wires across trees, breaks huge branches, and rips roofs. We were fortunate that there was no apparent damage, other than a few hours of peaceful silence while the electric company reconnected downed wires. Dick and I began a fearful "shall we mourn her loss?" pilgrimage to all Beauty's known haunts. No Beauty. No sightings. No peace. A few months later, Dick skipped up the front brick walk.

"Guess who I saw? Beauty is alive."

"Where? Are you sure?"

"Who else would do this? I opened the basement door and went inside. A few feet in, I turned to look at something, and there she was following my footsteps. When I reached down, she took off, but she didn't make any sounds of cooing and she flew crooked! It had to be her. Who else flies like that?"

So Beauty still lived, and we were able to easily spot her. She had a mate and occasionally she paid us a visit, walking in our garden and sitting on a feeder by my office window, staring at me with those beautiful dark eyes that said so much. It seems that all mourning doves treat us with the same friendship as Beauty. Anywhere we are, they don't fly away, they walk right near us. If they are feeding by my window and I open it, they continue with a little friendly nod.

The spirit of all is connected through the focus, intention, and actions we take. When life hands us unusual circumstances, we have an opportunity to discover and experience creation's infinite wisdom. Interspecies communication is stretching oneself into new regions of discovering possibilities. Choose to learn something totally new for you, something that threatens your comfort zone. It is a wonderful way to awaken the gifts. If you are facing challenges in your life, open the door to options. Make no absolutes about the way things have to be. Unconditional acceptance of our circumstances allows us to move forward without heavy emotional waves. Achieving the seemingly impossible begins by moving to the next moment without all the ands, ifs, and buts.

The Bronx Zoo in the 1950s was a scary place for me. Watching huge animals pace back and forth in a tiny cage made me cringe. It was easy to imagine how bored and depressed they must be. Separated from their own community and the familiar terrain of where they came from was horrific. If I had to be at a zoo because my parents believed I would somehow benefit from the experience, then the animals must benefit, too. I stood silently praying for them. After a few minutes, I would feel their attention turn towards me. I would send them love and friendship, telling them I am so very sorry humans did this to them. Before leaving I would tell them I'll always be their friend, please call on me when you need to be comforted and somehow I'll be there.

I certainly did not understand spirituality or metaphysics. It was painful to witness how humans could be so inconsiderate. I also did not know about rescuing endangered species, or what it took to create a healthy and safe environment for wildlife that needed a new home. I believe children are innocent until taught otherwise. Many children who felt as I did, grew up, and changed these prison-like zoos into what most of them are today. Animals who are endangered are now being rescued, and some of the species are recovering due to the inspired work of so many who care.

A friend of the family took us behind the scenes at Sea World where he was one of the curators. Sea turtles and manatees, each with huge bandages and their own little pool, were being nurtured and supported. One of Rick's jobs was to release these amazing creatures when they were completely healed. The manatees and the sea turtles were injured by boats.

We can all be healers. We can consciously focus our intention on being an instrument for a higher purpose. Let's imagine there is a frequency for each of our unique patterns of organic energy. There is the individual's frequency, and a frequency that connects all of life here and beyond that is Universal. Setting aside our personal frequency by asking to be channels for the highest good for all, creates an intentional focused connection with all of life. We truly become healers, letting the flow of life ripple through us, and into the pool of light frequency known as the healing energies.

If you see an animal injured and wish to help, you can go to the animal, or quiet down where you are. Completely immerse yourself in the role of healer. Trained rescue folks abound all over the world. When we are unsure, we can always reach out to find those who have done the work.

When your love and caring is far greater than your fear, your fear will depart. Injured animals can be frightening in their extreme vulnerability. So can people. You are the only person who can judge whether this is OK for you to do. If it is, then let the light of love guide your next moments. If at a distance, sit wherever you are, open your hands, palm upwards, ask our Creator to accept your offer to be a channel of healing, and then be one. Stay with this until a feeling becomes the message to stop.

Chapter 4

Dog Teachers & Others

All the lessons keep adding up for me. I have kept notes from 1974 on, hoping to make sense of what many ancient philosophies and religions spoke of, that we are all connected. Some feel that only those that think or believe as they do, are connected, not the others. I believe that is what creates the disconnect that can lead to abuse. I remember a time when I discovered some children are taught by their elders that animals have no soul. That makes it easy to dismiss the feelings both of the animal and other people. It gets easier to love all creatures, when we seek to know the soul of each being we encounter. I love turning to the birds, chipmunks, and squirrels for friendship. Knowing we share a planet that is filled with both troubles and great miracles, I focus more on the miracles. Walking a dog is no longer an option for me; and our wondrous Sammy, our last cat, left this earth at age twenty-one. I can still sit outside and meet friends like Tink the chipmunk, who will not take any food from a bowl. He sits on my lap and waits to be hand fed. One squirrel was curious, watching the chipmunks put two and three unshelled peanuts in their mouths. That squirrel refuses to leave after one peanut. She patiently waits for the second one, since she learned how to get two in her mouth. A blue jay was watching the chipmunk and the squirrel. Now that blue jay also waits for the second peanut and manages two in his or her beak!

Tink waiting to be hand fed.

Tink was not the first chipmunk to be friends with us. Several years before, we had four cats, Sammy, Kit, Kaboodle, and Boo Girl. One day a chipmunk sat in our living room. The cats were resting, job done. They invited this new friend to live with us. The chipmunk ate out of a tiny British ceramic butter dish for about three months. Warmer weather came and the chipmunk left for greener pastures, and probably back to its own hollow.

Around the same time, we kept finding peanuts everywhere in our home, under baseboards, in the stove drawer, and other absurd places. Coming home one day, we opened the front door to see a squirrel seated on our couch munching on peanuts. The cats looked like they were smiling. Apparently new friends were important to them. Sammy was the culprit, as we soon saw her sitting with the squirrel. She loved all other life forms, except a young fox. At twenty-one years of age, Sammy chased the poor frightened fox off from our deck with a screech of anger. The poor little guy ran off terrified. Running to see if she was alright, I saw my sweet baby girl turn into a fierce warrior. No wonder the fox ran away.

Years ago, we put leftover food and nuts outside our back door. We soon discovered a mommy raccoon bringing her babies to eat. She would wait a few feet away from them. There they were, three little raccoons and Needleteeth. The raccoons would fight for the food with each other. They never touched Needleteeth, an adorable opossum, their Mom's adopted child. When we see how different species adopt babies from other species, love them, nurture and feed them, we can see how love is truly the universal language.

For many years I would spend a week in Saratoga Springs, New York, on the campus of Skidmore College. It was the site for the annual conference of the International Women's Writing Guild. I first met the founder of the IWWG at a gathering in NYC. Upon meeting, she said "you need to join my new organization and come with us to our yearly event." I may have nodded, wondering why I would go, since I did not consider myself a writer. Hannelore Hahn, the founder, persisted. She would call me for a psychic reading, and then mention the week-long retreat held in the summer. I probably muttered something about being busy.

One day after chatting on the phone, she firmly stated "I want you to come this August to our retreat."

"Hannelore I need a lot more notice than a month."

"Fine, next August." She then rattled off dates. I was cornered. Then she continued "and you will teach!"

"What will I teach!?"

Laughing she countered, "using your psychic gifts!"

What she did not know was I could not afford the weeklong costs. With her invitation to teach, it was all free! I might be able to learn how to write. Having taken a lot of notes while working with law enforcement, it was the first thing I thought. Maybe I could write and help others with their journey. In between classes I gave there, I took classes on writing fiction, nonfiction, grant writing, and so much more. They were remarkable teachers, every single one of them. In one class, we were asked what the subject of our book would be. I could only think of what I knew that might be unusual, being a psychic detective. After I spoke, the teacher then said, "nice fiction idea."

I corrected her with, "It's nonfiction, it's my work." Suddenly everyone was commenting that they couldn't wait to hear more. I was hooked.

If I had not taken notes when I worked with law enforcement, I could not have written the first draft of my nonfiction book. It has taken many years of stumbling to finally be comfortable writing more than a blog. Record or write your own tuning in. You never know how useful it may become in the future.

One summer Sandy Van Hoose (now Sandy Van Hoose Saunders) came to my workshop at the Guild and signed up for a psychic reading. She was, and still is. vibrant, outgoing, and creative. We quickly struck up a friendship. This is not unusual at the Guild; by the end of the week we all went home with friendships deepened, new bonds created, and inspiration to write, write, write. Sandy called me in November months after saying goodbye.

"Remember you told me that in November I would get news from the West Coast, and that I would do something out there around Christmas that would change my life? I sent a letter to the NBC show 'The Other Side' about my standard poodle named Murphe, being the reincarnation of my previous dog, a Great Dane named Murphy. They just called me. They're in Los Angeles and they want to fly me out around Christmas for the taping of a show on animals. I just wanted you to know. Do you ever work with animals?"

Now, that is funny for me, since I always see the connection between my supposedly varied careers. Sandy and I had spoken about her dog, but I hadn't thought it necessary to use my abilities in that direction. There was nothing wrong, and Murphe wasn't missing.

Sandy had a wonderful experience about which she had written "Love Returns." Sandy sent the story to the producers of "The Other Side."

Her beloved Great Dane had always skipped one of the front steps (the same one every time) as he bounded up to the front door. After he passed away, Sandy searched for another Great Dane. When her brother's standard poodle gave birth, Sandy felt it was the right one, sight unseen, many states away, and claimed it as her own. Upon picking up her young, new friend, he promptly fell asleep on her lap on the way home. When arriving at her home, he stopped at the same step, jumped over it, and, headed to the favorite spot of her previous friend! He's been doing it ever since.

She said, "I'm going to call the producer and ask if they would want some information on you. I'll call you back."

She called, and then they did. With my plane ticket in hand, I kissed my children and left for the West Coast, with the knowledge that I could still celebrate the holidays back home. Two days before Christmas, Sandy and I met in Los Angeles, at the hotel the film producers had reserved. A delightful dinner was shared, and then we went to her room where Murphe was staying. He was a beautiful black standard poodle. Sweet and friendly, his heart was very certain that Sandy and he were soul kin.

Murphe with Sandy and Nancy

The next day, we were taken to the studio. Walking through the corridors, we met Jay Leno on his way to work, and Mel Torme finishing work. (Google if you don't know him.) Waiting in a huge green room, we were asked to sit about twenty feet away from a big beautiful Rottweiler, Queenie, with her buddy, a man in his thirties. Curious, I asked George, the guy sitting next to her, why we weren't allowed near. George was a firefighter, and the happy companion to a male Rottweiler, who he took out every Sunday for a hike in the mountains. He had saved another firefighter's life, and as a thank you he was gifted with this female, Queenie, who promptly settled in as a family member. One Sunday the three of them were hiking up a mountain when the female sat down and refused to budge. She then started tugging to get them back down. They followed her lead. Once in the door of the home, George promptly collapsed with a heart attack. The female Rottie quickly got a phone and pushed the handle (landline) to his hand. He was barely able to call for help. Ready to pass out, the dogs kept him awake by licking his face, pushing his head lightly, and with paws pumping his chest a bit. When the EMTs arrived, he was able to call the dogs off. They would have attacked anyone attempting to come near him, unless they heard his command. They knew that! That is why they kept him awake. Queenie was listening intently as he concluded with telling us, she is more protective than ever.

Think of all she understood that was not evident before the event, even to George. He couldn't feel what was going on with his own body, but she could!

George and Queenie left to go tell their story to the waiting audience. After that, it was our turn. The show was put together by believers, from the audio engineers to the host. It was a sweet and loving experience.

Since then many have asked, "Was I with my dog, cat, or horse in a past life?" Or, "Will my … come back to me in another form soon?" If you have ever wondered about your relationship with an animal, past, present, or future, now is the time to practice!

A local nonprofit rescue association had given a couple my name and number. They had just adopted a rescue dog of mixed breed. They were warned that the dog had been barking and trying to bite everybody at the kennel. They were told if you have any problem continuing, just call Nancy. They called and were hesitant to bring the dog. I told them to just keep the dog on a leash when they come. At that time I had two cats who loved sleeping on the couch by the front door. The couple and dog entered the living room. The cats looked up, yawned, and went right back to sleep. The dog stood still and silent. He continued to stay there quietly as I introduced, imagining that our souls were beaming love to each other. That took seconds, after which they followed me to my office down the hall. The three of them followed me. I closed the door to the office and suggested they take his leash off. It was obvious that they were very nervous about his behavior. Once the leash was off, he meandered a little bit, found a nice space, and lay down and went to sleep. The look on their faces was fun for me to watch.

"It's not magic. Your friend has been exhausted by all the toxins he keeps smelling in the house. Dogs' olfactory sense is many times stronger than ours. Scent, for all of us, goes faster to the brain than any other sense. Scent has a chemical structure that affects the brain. Try driving with windows open near a plant that emits sulfur into the air. Nausea, gasping for breath—those are the brain's warning of toxin-causing problems. My home is completely free of false fragrances and any other toxins, hopefully. It's low in toxicity, and that is why he can finally rest. When you are home, you may want to take a few of your household products and a couple of your personal care products, like your soap and shampoo, and look up the ingredients. Read by looking at the dangers of those ingredients. Your dog is the canary in the coal mine."

A canary in a coal mine is an advanced warning of some danger. The metaphor originates from the times when miners used to carry caged canaries while at work; if there was any methane or carbon monoxide in the mine, the canary would die before the levels of the gas reached those hazardous to humans. The humans would be able to quickly leave.

Dogs are scent specific; A dog's acuity to a scent group is so refined that they are able to discriminate humans by odor and can even match certain scents to specific body parts of an individual. Their olfactory systems have far more receptors than ours; we have about five thousand, dogs average fifty-five thousand, and cats about ten thousand. Domesticated animals need natural scent—nothing adulterated and no synthetics. Knowing what is real is more difficult when looking online. Marketing can be misleading. Intuition and looking behind the buzz words to the truth takes work. One simple way to discover the difference between real scent that comes from healthy soil, whether farmed or wild crafted, is to just call any essential oil company to see if you can visit their farms. I've been to two in the United States, one in Canada, and one in Ecuador. A close friend who lives in Spain has been to the same companies' farms in France, Spain, and Croatia. Talking with the farmers and those in charge of the distilleries, I am humbled by what nature provides. If you are told you cannot see a farm (after the pandemic lockdown), ask why. The company I chose has been a blessing in my life and those of my pets, family, friends, clients, and more. It is because of the efficacy of the farmer who created this incredible legacy for everyone's well-being. It is beneficial for all species with the exception of some insects—mosquitos, wasps, and a few others I'm happy to say avoid me. If you have wasps nearby, grab some peppermint or spearmint leaves, crunch them to release the oil's scent, and keep them with you. The wasps won't go near.

Take a walk in nature if you can. Consciously open your heart and mind to be receptive to all of nature. Send a message to the forest, the ocean, the sand, your backyard—wherever you are. Notice how you felt before and then after connecting. A fun vision I created years ago, and still play with, is to see myself stepping outside my door and having the trees, birds, sky, land, and all, greet me as I ponder their glory.

Creator of all life, my soul reaches for the light, and through the light I reach out to all others. All of life is my family, and I thank you for this opportunity to engage my expanded family in conversation.

Believe your statement. Believe and be receptive. If you feel inclined to stop and watch an insect or listen to a bird, that is the member of your family who is responding to your message. Start talking like Pat did with Innish.

We met Innish on June 27, 2002 when visiting my husband's good friend, Pat. Pat is an easy-going man who Dick would often drop at his place of business. They met as engineers in the same field of development years before. Both have a deep affection and love for all species. Dick (my husband) had seen Pat the previous week. He suggested I might want to meet his new dog, Innish.

We parked our car right outside the glass door entrance to Pat's business. Before getting out, I wanted to ease the tension between us. We were having a discussion, both upset over problems with one of our children, differing in our approach.

"We need to be connected, flowing with the energy. Let's find a way."

That was my need speaking. I knew meeting a dog, they are sensitive to everyone's energy. A beautiful black and white springer spaniel sat looking at us from inside the door. As we opened it, he began a low growl.

Pat looked at Innish and said, "That's odd; he didn't growl at Dick last week."

I responded, "He wouldn't, he's not afraid of men, only women, women who hold any tension."

"Yes, that's true. He growls at my daughter, and she loves him."

"But she's having a difficult time right now that is causing her some stress."

"Yes, she is."

"Okay, when the problem is gone, and she learns to clear her stress rather than carry it, Innish will feel safe."

We then proceeded to a room where we could all sit. Innish did not leave Pat's side, and Pat did not stop peacefully stroking him.

"I see a woman with a stick, she's lifting it up to hit. Innish received lots and lots of beatings, was starved a lot, and was never allowed in the house?" I am never sure of what I get until there is some feedback.

49

Pat filled us in. "I knew the neighbor of the owners of Innish. It was a shovel that she hit Innish and his brothers over the head with, again and again. They were chained up outside for breeding purposes only. The neighbor called me when she knew that two of the dogs had died from starvation. She told me the dogs were never let in the house. The owners of the house went away during the winter, and left the dogs to starve. Everyone was afraid of the owners, who would suddenly pop up to apparently get something inside the house. I went every day of the week for one week. I sat opposite him most of the day, leaving bits of food through the chain-link fence. By the sixth day, I attempted to get Innish to go with me. He simply accepted me. He came to work with me that day and every day since. He lives with me and is a great friend. He's incredibly bright. I've never had to housebreak him; he automatically understood. I can tell him to stay, I'll be right back, and he does."

Pat never changes his inflection or tone, no hand signals, just conversation with a dog that completely understands him. I lay down near Innish and peacefully centered myself. I could feel Innish's past tensions slipping away. Innish took my hand with his paw, and motioned for me to put my hand under his head. He peacefully closed his eyes as he lay on my hand.

When we were ready to leave, Pat casually told Innish to go to his office. "I'll be right back."

Innish got up, and promptly walked down the hall into the office, where he lay down to wait. The remarkable wisdom of Innish had come through clearly. His soul remained a great teacher, showing how to love and trust in spite of abuse issues. His energy and health became wonderful despite his past. Knowing this, I believe he knew the depth of loss of his own kin, yet lived with the willingness to restore his trust in humans. He knew discernment, and could trust with all his heart and soul.

Several encounters with pain-ridden, frightened, angry animals have taught me that coming from the heart not only makes it safe, it can also create miracles. One of them was a big shaggy dog. Meeting my girlfriend to go out for lunch, she asked if I would mind helping a friend of hers.

"Her dog has a problem. We pass their home on the way to the restaurant, so can we stop there?"

"Sure, just remember, I don't want to know what the problem is."

Pulling into her friend's driveway, we saw the woman opening her front door. Out bounded this 100 or so pounds of shaggy fur. I was so happy to see this huge baby, that I ran out to greet her or him (remember, I only knew it was a dog). I plopped onto the front lawn and she (turned out to be a female) rolled on the grass exposing her belly for me to rub. We played for a few minutes, and then happily collapsed together, dog in my lap, my face in her fur. All along I was conscious that despite her appearance she needed a very gentle touch. There was absolute silence around us. Finally the woman who opened the door spoke.

"How did you do that?"

"Do what?"

"Get Jasmine to play?"

"What's so hard?"

"Well, we needed your help because she attacks everyone but me!"

"She's just afraid of how people handle her. She has a lot of joint pain. Hasn't the vet talked with you?"

"Yes, in fact we were told she's got arthritis."

"Well, if your joints were as swollen and painful as hers, you'd be scared of being touched except by those who know how to touch you."

The rest of the meeting was spent discussing ways to assist at home. Ditching all toxic cleaners both in the home and the family's personal care products would help unburden Jasmine's body, along with other natural tools to ease some of the body's burden. Showing her how she could use a healing touch. By thinking of the energy as universal going through her when caring for another, is different than using her own energy. When I got up, Jasmine stood with me.

I turned to the mom with "Think of a battery needing charging. We don't use our own battery to charge another. We use something that connects between both—that's universal!"

When we left, Jasmine tried to join us. Knowing the restaurant would not accommodate her, we had a good kiss, both of us trotting off to our individual worlds.

The more you practice hands-on healing, the more available and sensitive you become to the energy fields. Keep a log of your experiences. Trust any thoughts, words that pop up in your mind, and sensations you experiences. Jot them down. It takes a while to recognize the subtle messages, particularly with all our expectations, and brain jams on *how could a dog possibly tell me something in my language?* They don't. This is an amazing and complex universe. Think about how your body translates information constantly from food particles and air temperatures. Does your body talk? In English or French? There is a language that is truly universal, a language not of the tongue but of the energy fields that surround and permeate all of life. The energy is a transformer, with the junctions being each individual cell of existence. It's happening all the time, nonstop. Now, how easy is it to understand a parrot or a cat or an elephant? If billions of bits of information are constantly streaming through us, the trick is not to learn to tune in, it is to learn to quiet down enough to focus on one tiny bit among the billions. Your other species friend will love for you to truly understand what would help improve the relationship between the two of you. Once you start tuning in, you may suddenly decide to read about nutrition and pets, homeopathy, aromatherapy, reiki, shiatsu, and on and on. Who is the teacher and who is the student?

Taking that leap of faith to believe I can translate the information coming from one specific individualized field of energy known as Coco-Nut (a rescued bird) or Quinnie (I was aunt to this fabulous golden retriever), took repeated suspension of my doubts and fears. When you suddenly think, *feed her a carrot, how strange, why would I feed her a carrot,* go and feed her the carrot. When your dog eagerly chomps down, wags her tail and finishes the carrot, stop and realize you just received a clear message and responded. Note the milestone. Now, there will be many more, so many that one day you will look back and vaguely recall how it was not to feel connected to all other sentient life.

"Hi, what a nice dog. How old is she?"

Ever say that? Next time you are out somewhere and see a dog you like, ask the dog with your inside voice, "How old are you?" A number will pop up in your head. Now you can ask the person walking with dog, "How old is she?" Or if you want, do what I do:

"Hi, your dog is beautiful. Is she four?"

"No, she's three."

"Hmm, she seems to be four."

"Let's see. She was born in...right, of course, she just turned four. Yes, she is beautiful. Have a great day."

Most people don't notice, or are too polite to ask, how I know. Try it. You might have lots of fun and get to know some great animals. Every year for 15 years I attended and given workshops for the International Women's Writing Guild's Annual Conference. It was held in Saratoga Springs, New York, at Skidmore College. While wandering on one of the campus paths, my girlfriend Judi (proud mom of Quinnie), and I saw a beautiful big golden retriever sitting near a man. The man was seated on a bench holding the dog's leash. I walked over as I kept up a running mental message with the dog. *I don't know why you are anxious or uncomfortable. Can I help in any way?* As soon as I approached, the dog lay down and held up one leg.

"Tommy, what are you doing?" the dog's best friend said.

"I think he just wants me to know where his problem is."

"He's going for surgery on his leg in two days. That's odd, why would he show it to you?"

"I work with animals. Maybe he knows that."

"Yes, I suppose, but it is so odd, that he is still showing you his leg."

"He wants me to put my hands on him. Would that be all right with you?"

"Sure."

With my hands, I touched his injured area gently. With my soul, I prayed for a successful outcome. When I felt done, I stood up. Tommy regained his seated posture, licked my hand, and put his head under my palm. I continued to send him positive thoughts, and promised him my spirit would be with him throughout the next few days. He wagged his tail.

I've noticed throughout the years that if you come from love and sincerity, most people will not question your motives. They will feel your integrity and allow you to move into their lives for a while. All the fears of what others may think of as weird are simply our own insecurities talking to us. Over the years mine have diminished to a whimper.

Several days passed and Judi and I took a walk into town along Broadway. We loved the homes that reminded me of the film *Somewhere in Time*. Huge, graceful entries welcoming guests, gardens dressed to the nines, with an array of floral scents. Once in town we saw Tommy and his favorite human. Tommy wagged his tail and showed us a big happy smile. I can remember animal names better than I remember most humans. Tommy's buddy spoke:

"The vet was surprised at how well Tommy did. He appeared happy to be there, and once it was done he licked everyone he could to thank them. Look at him now. It's like nothing ever happened!"

> *If you pick up a starving dog and make him prosperous he will not bite you. This is the principal difference between a dog and man.* —Mark Twain

Infinite intelligence takes the form of a human, a cat, a dog, a fly, a bird. That is my recall of a passage in *Kinship with All Life*. Think of your own experience. Discovering another species' ability to catch your attention. We are not alone in our intelligence and wisdom.

It is always easier to change our routines and habits, when we are not desperate to change them. If you are not in the midst of overwhelming crisis, find the time each day to practice intentional sending and receiving of love. If you are in the midst of too much tension to ground yourself, then select a coach, a mentor, someone to whom you will listen, to guide you inside. Communication happens best in a state of calm love. So many strangers dressed in feathers, fur, or gills have helped me in moments of despair. One furry friend helped solve a missing children case! By rescuing her, she helped solve a burglary at my home and then find three missing children!!! What a truly angelic dog Ramona was. I love that lady and miss her precious self. While her body was partially a mess, broken from being hit by a car and then dumped by her owners, she came to us with seizures, and a trusting heart. She became the best friend for my family and the mother of three children who had been missing. That story is in my book, *The Life of a Psychic Detective*.

One of the first steps I took was to create a simple method to relax yet be alert. I remember in nursing we learned to observe a patient' breathing rate—whether it was shallow or full expansion like a baby's. They warned us that we can unconsciously join them in that style of breathing. If theirs is shallow, we can consciously take slow, deep breaths. We would then notice that the person joins us in deeper breathing. Everyone around relaxes. That works with wildlife and pets. Our worries and fears are easily transmitted. So are peace, happiness, and joy. I used that practice to start me off.

Many of you already practice some sort of relaxation technique, yet in today's fast pace we can forget. If you need a reminder or simply want to get started, here's a quick take. Place yourself in a position where you can be comfortable, without restricting your circulation and flow of oxygen.

Place pillows wherever you need to relieve tension, or sit with your back straight, head centered (please look in a mirror once to check yourself out), and again keep arms and legs uncrossed. Loosen all restrictive clothing. Relax and deep breathe first into your belly, then your chest. Exhale slower than you inhale. This is a simple method to cleanse your lungs. With every breath you take, send a command to your body, instructing it to let go of tension. Play with seeing or feeling light as a spectrum of colors dancing through your whole being. At www.nancyorlenweber.com on a blog of *More Gifts of Music For Everyone,* play the "World Within." My voice and the music can temporarily assist you until you can do it on your own.

When you are comfortable with learning to relax, you can be standing in the middle of Grand Central Station or facing a crazed, raging beast (or person), and get through the moment without harming your own body through an extreme response. Keep yourself centered, so you can trust whether to stay in a situation or, as my karate sensei once said, run like hell. Clarity allows us to feel calm, and emotionally unattached to the outcome. We only need the fight or flight rush of adrenaline for actual situations. It can be fatigued through extreme and constant negative thinking, reliving fear-driven memories. We can see that in some pets we rescue, who have been so harmed that they are either hyper-vigilant or lack in energy. That's why prayer, meditation, and all that allows us to be truly here matters. I learned in nursing school that if we are peaceful, then even the butterfly will be our friend, landing gently on us to say hello. I love sending to all wildlife and domesticated animal a simple prayer; from my soul, my heart, to yours, through the light of the one who created us all. I offer you my love, strength and joy at knowing of your existence. I wish you good health and a long life. Please call on me so that I may be of service. Thank you for letting me join with you for the moment.

Chapter 5

Missing Animals are my Teachers

Sometimes, having no idea consciously on how to do something, the heart knows how to compel us to take the risk. Moving from Peekskill, New York to Budd Lake, New Jersey, I was hoping to continue my work as a medical intuitive, medium, and more. Those are simply words defining aspects of the same light, focused in different directions. Until I became unable to walk much, I was able to dance nonstop, except when the musicians took a break. It was common for someone to approach me and ask, "Where do you get your energy?" I would point upwards and smile. When anyone approached me to converse, eventually the question was "What do you do?" My answer was, and is, "I follow the guidance from within that comes to me from our Creator."

"No, I mean what do you *do?*"

I would smile, shrug, laugh, and dance some more. The work has always been about listening to that which knows far more than I ever will. Listening inside, then outside.

I read somewhere that the universe is our mirror. More than anything, I wanted to relieve suffering—first mine, then others. I began diving into psychology and psychiatry at about age nine. By the sixth grade, I was writing a brief history of insane asylums as my year-end paper. I wanted to take my own pain and transform it into something creative, something that would stop the looping over the past. I continued the excursion and realized that by having almost no memory loss, it was easy to pull on the threads of what events took my innocence and bashed it to smithereens. The voice of a spirit I knew since birth, shared lovingly that, while I was painfully shy, and very introverted, a transformation would happen if I continued my search. I wanted to understand, and still search out, why humans will hurt and even kill their own species. I remember how I felt when I found out that there are people who hunt and kill strictly for sport. Having believed that I could hear lobster scream, I have never eaten one. Seeing a fish hooked, I cried, believing that they feel pain. The article I later read, on fish and pain, for those who are curious is at https://www.smithsonianmag.com/science-nature/fish-feel-pain-180967764/.

I realize that each of us makes a choice, either conscious or unconscious. My husband, who is my beloved soulmate, eats fish, chicken and turkey. His blood type is O-positive, and according to what he thinks, he needs it. Most of my friends eat healthy organic foods, and are not vegans or vegetarians. We all need to make our choices consciously according to our beliefs. I grew up eating meat. I started to question it one day, when my mother was cooking something called tongue.

"What's that?"

"It's tongue," my mother said, obviously annoyed at the interruption.

I persisted. "What do you mean?"

"Cow's tongue."

I wouldn't eat it. Like many, I am extremely visual in my mind. I cringed, then thought of the others she cooked. I began to rebel, quietly, afraid of more yelling from my mother.

I didn't make complete changes until I stopped needing approval from others. That took quite a while. Having a mother terrified of anything that moves except for humans, we had one puppy my sister named Susie.

My sister was able to trick our mother into keeping Susie. After four years, mother left it at a kill shelter. I vowed to have all the animals I wanted when living on my own. I believe Susie is one of the inspirations for helping all other creatures.

Teaching psychic development and meditation in the 1970s on Thursday evenings, was created by clients asking me to teach. One of them owned a horse. Anne came in a bit late, apologizing that "my horse is acting weird." I drew a line on a paper and marked one area with an X. That was a first for me. I could not draw a horse, so a wiggly line represented the spine.

"Anne, pretend this is the horse's spine. About two-thirds down the back, I sense a problem by the vertebrae."

"Would you mind if I call the barn? I left someone there to watch him."

When she spoke to the woman attending the horse, she quickly got a big yes. Upon lightly touching that area, the horse started rearing up.

"What do we do?"

Anne wanted the next piece, and I knew it was not something I consciously knew. As a student nurse in Brooklyn College, my first teacher, Mrs. Norman, taught us a great lesson.

"When you enter the room to serve, put all your troubles and concerns in a bag by the door. When you leave the room you can pick them up, if you still want to."

That's just what I did when I let go of my fears: "Anne, if you have any natural massage oil, ask the woman to gently apply it, by creating a large circle with her palms all around that area. Then have her fingers go to the muscles on each side, using firm yet slight pressure, to massage the muscles."

The woman called back fifteen minutes later. Keeping myself glued to the class agenda, I was content giving whatever I could, not expecting or rejecting what might happen. Anne hung up with a big smile, and said

"Thank you, it worked!" I was surprised and curious. Could I help other animals? It was one of the early peeks into how else I could serve.

When I began to work with animals, it was natural that once in a while someone would ask about a missing or deceased pet. Again, I was in unfamiliar terrain. Putting aside my concern that I was totally unschooled in finding animals, once again I leaped into the situation eager to discover if I could be of any use.

A client called from the Northwest of the United States. With a distraught tone, she told her story. She had a pack of trail dogs that go with her and her horse. The lead dog had suddenly left the trail and never came back. That was three months ago. I smiled as I heard her. My heart feeling was that the lead dog was not only fine, he was super smart, and knew while he would miss her and that life, he had a new one that he also loved. I passed that along, knowing it was hard for her to believe it. She called me about nine months later excited to share.

"Yesterday I saw him on the hilltop outside my home. He was with a wolf and their cubs! He's married!"

When we hung up, I could still feel her elation and wonder at what she had just learned. A dog's body houses a soul with a yearning for its own heritage, a family. Years before I spoke with her, I had read, *Never Cry Wolf: Amazing True Story of Life Among Arctic Wolves*, by Farley Mowat in 2001 (published decades after the events in the book), who was assigned as a naturalist by the Canadian Wildlife Service to investigate why wolves were killing Arctic caribou. Mowat's account of the summer he lived on the frozen tundra alone, studying the wolf population, and developing a deep affection for the wolves (who were of no threat to caribou or man), and for a friendly Inuit tribe known as the Ihalmiut ("People of the Deer"), was remarkable. One incident he recounted left an indelible impression on me. An Inuit who could understand the language of the wolves, was looking at a wolf den with Farley. He saw the male "talking" with his wife. He turned to Farley and told him:

"He tells her he is going hunting and will be back at noon tomorrow."

At noon the next day, he returned. That stayed with me. I wanted to hear everything: what does a bird's trill mean, how do my feline and canine buddies speak, howls mean what, and I know trees are alive, so they too have some form of communication. Then I remembered another amazing piece of news, written in a daily newspaper in the late 1970s. Mt. Sinai Hospital had reported on a specific mutation of a bacteria and at the same exact day of discovery so did a Russian hospital report the same form of mutation with the same bacteria. Today's wireless world is a reproduction of what already exists among all species. All life communicates in some fashion, but very little of it is understood by humans.

When someone read an article referencing how I found missing animals, one of those who called opened memories of my own German shepherd, who had been on the other side for many years. The woman's voice was spilling frantically through the wire, as she implored me to find her dog. Bunny was possibly stolen, and she was desperate.

"What is your name?"

"Sue Parks. I'm sorry, but I'm absolutely desperate. Bunny means everything to me. I can't get around well. It's hard to go looking. I found your name in *Grit* magazine. You do find missing pets, don't you?"

"Sometimes. I'll do whatever I can to help."

My hand still held the telephone and my feet still touched the floor; something I call my essence was no longer in Budd Lake, New Jersey. I was traveling with the winds, faster than I could be aware of. Seconds ago, Sue asked a question, and now I was staring out through the eyes of a beautiful, sweet German Shepherd with my vision on Sue's dog, it triggered a memory of the first dog I had as an adult. I couldn't stop the memory.

It was 1968; I was pregnant, married to Dr. Gilbert Arnold Preston. We lived in Puerto Rico while my husband did research on split-brain functions. A year later my daughter was born. My OB/GYN, a navy physician called me after I gave birth, asking if I could take a German shepherd puppy, Galt. He was five months old. His children were abusive to the puppy. He was concerned that this little guy was beginning to bite. Agreeing, I prepared by being ready to walk around with towels wrapped around my hands. When he tried to bite me, he got a mouthful of towel. With love and a tone that showed him I was sad, for what he went through, he calmed right down. Mary and her little lamb never had it so good. He didn't need training. We were inseparable from the first. Within a month, he and my three-month-old daughter were happily bonded.

Puerto Rico 1969 German Shepherd loving Rebecca

My then-husband hated the dog's being in our bed. As soon as he shut the door behind him to go to work, my buddy jumped in, and put his head on the empty pillow next to mine. That sweet young dog died from extensive hemorrhaging at eleven months of age. It led to my research. Gil hated roaches, so he used a roach bomb. I had no knowledge back then of what it could do. I later learned that it was the roach bomb that caused Galt to die. While the lesson was a horrible one, at a cost of a life, I have learned that helping others save their pets' lives, is what I can do. In love and honoring his life, I research everything, and then I research some more.

A few years later, I was living in Peekskill, New York. Louisa Poole, an artist, Tarot reader, numerologist, and so much more, came down from Rockport, Massachusetts to teach my students. At night we would sit for hours, chatting about our mutual perceptions of the universe.

One morning while outside, she remarked, "You always have this German shepherd at your side. He never leaves you."

That's my precious soul kin. It's so easy to feel both how much I miss him, and how much I love him. Tears and smiles bind us together. Now gone many years, Galt and Bunny were joined in my heart. Bunny seemed to have the same depth of devotion and sweetness. I ached for her.

What seemed like a long time was probably no more than a minute when I responded to Sue's voice on the phone again asking what I saw.

The thoughts and vision came easily as I answered Sue. "The first thing I see is Bunny in Virginia. I see her being taken in a station wagon. There are two men in it. They feel like they just pulled a robbery. She is with a man with a shotgun. He is scuzzy looking. I see him on top of a hill."

Flustered Sue responded with "That's impossible. My car was stolen, but she's definitely not in Virginia. I live in Maryland, but I'm not near Virginia. That's quite a run. She can't be there." Sue voiced her frustration. "Please, I need your help. Can't you tell me anything else."

Again I closed my eyes searching for another vision. Then, "You had a station wagon?"

"Yes,"

"Then I do see it. It's the first town over the border, going directly south from you. I can only tell you what I see. Bunny is a large German shepherd, isn't she?"

Now Sue was quieter when she responded. "Yes, that's true."

"Then it's her I'm seeing. Call me again when you get any lead on the car or just to talk. I'll see if more comes." I hung up not expecting any results.

The call came the next day. Breathless with anxiety, Sue began, "Bunny was seen in a station wagon heading south after a robbery with two men driving. The police think they were heading toward Virginia. How did you know? When will they find her? Is she okay?"

"Yes, Bunny is not hurt, but she'll be hungry and scared. I don't see the men harming her."

"How can you be sure?"

"I'm traveling there with my mind; that's how I can tell. Sue, I've been like this ever since I can remember. I'm so glad Bunny has you. You must love each other very much. Thanks for calling and keeping me informed. I'll be praying for her. Keep sending her loving thoughts. Keep your fears away from your thoughts of her. It's important. She's very telepathic; loving you, she is very sensitive to your thoughts."

"But how am I ever going to get her back? Where is she? She can't be in Virginia."

"Why don't you send me a photo of her? In the meantime, until I get it, please work on letting some of the fear abate and remaining open to the possibilities I'm seeing. I could be wrong, I could also be right. Call me in a day or two."

The photos were on my desk two days later when her call came.

"Hi, Sue. Okay, this time I see her by railroad tracks. Wait a minute; I think I feel a name coming...Harper's Ferry, West Virginia. Isn't that a movie or something?"

"Are you sure?"

"Yes. Hold on, there are more images coming. I'm waiting for them to clear."

The images were barely there. They were like looking through a long tunnel, to see a speck of something. Only you know the speck is the key to a mystery, and it's important to get a detail shot, somehow enlarge it, and translate it into common sense and be right.

"There are mountains and water nearby. She's on a mountain, alone. She's waiting for you. You can find her. Sue, you are going to see a truck, wooden sides, color green, and there's a bandanna on the seat."

"Is that where Bunny is?"

"No, but it's a clue to tell you that you are on the right track. I think she is by the railroad tracks near the mountain. Poor girl, she misses you. You've been sending her a lot of good messages. I can feel her being comforted."

Sue called back with the good news. Bunny was in her arms again. I turned to Galt, now many years a spirit: "Thanks for keeping Bunny company. I love you. Just once more I'd love to hug you. You kept me company in some of my darkest moments."

All beings tremble before violence. All fear death, all love life.
See yourself in others. Then whom can you hurt? What harm
can you do? —Buddha

If you are curious, treat your intuition with respect. Take index cards, a journal, or store info on your device. Keep it with you at all times. The instant flash of intuition occurs in a seemingly random way. Just keep programming to be available. When you do notice a sudden out-of-the-blue image, thought, sensation, word, and so on, note it down, and record the date. Trust that it means something. You may have to interpret its meaning, or it may be clear and direct. Even when it appears clear, it can still be a metaphor. Seeing death isn't always a literal, clear vision; it can, and usually does mean the end of something as you know it.

Teachers come in all sizes and all ages. Scripture tells us "out of the mouths of babes." I've since included puppies, kittens and all the innocent of the planet as filled with wisdom, too. I've learned through those missing, those gone from physical life, and the wonderful ability of the innocent to openly share their journey with other species. Many are lost; some I could help find; and others I have no idea what happened. I found it important to just do the work, and pray that all ends well. Because Bunny and

65

some others I helped caught the attention of the newspapers, including the *National Enquirer*. I was swamped with calls asking to find people's loved ones. Overwhelmed, I sought to refer to anyone that I believed could do the work. One situation caught my attention, and I ended up flying to California. It was the devotion the two men had to their dog, and their need to have any insight. Unfortunately, I believed the dog was stolen. It turned out to be true, and the thieves got a great deal of money when they sold the dog back to the owners.

Then a call came from a friend of a friend, frantically spilling out the story of a friendly terrier who was his pal. Owning his own store, he took him to work every day. Suddenly the six-year-old dog was nowhere to be found. I mentioned the next town east of theirs. He hung flyers in his town and one east. Days went by when he received a call saying, "Your dog was so friendly, I thought it was local. I invited him in for a snack, and he came right in. After some food, he walked out. I'm sorry I didn't know he was lost."

For 364 days, I could track him town by town. He was going in a spiral and he was slowly coming back to the starting point. All the calls that came in were similar to the first. On the 365th day he showed up at his buddy's door wagging his tail.

I told the dog's friend, "He wanted an adventure, he is not a baby, he's an adult who likes to explore."

I am so glad I keep notes. I have told many of my classes a very condensed version of the Dobie story. That is because I didn't read my notes! While reading the notes, I discovered how much I had forgotten. I don't like fooling myself into believing something about me is true. It's why I started taking notes on everything going through my thoughts, gut instinct, images that would pop up, and more. I would date them, and if needed draw the picture I saw. Unfortunately, I couldn't draw most of my life until I finally picked up a book *Drawing with the Right Side of the Brain*. After that, I could at least do something resembling the image.

It was late October 1988.

Sandy had a 12-week-old dobermann pinscher puppy, who she brought back from a dog show in California. Donald, Sandy's closest friend, trained her dogs. He was gravely ill, and asked her to take care of this puppy. They were both professional dog handlers. Sandy hoped that by buying the puppy, Donald might believe that he would be around in two years. The puppy would be old enough at that point to show.

Sandy bought the dog to her home, in the middle of nowhere, isolated, nearly one thousand acres, bounded by the Patische River. The river suddenly stops its course and goes around, surrounding this acreage. Sandy and her husband live at the head of the acreage. She had an older female, Dobie, who never gets lost. One Sunday morning at 9:00 a.m., Sandy, her dog, and the puppy took to the main roads, to help the little dog familiarize himself with his surroundings. Sandy's faithful companion, Astin, who was ten years old, was running ahead with the little puppy following her.

Astin, knowing the area very well, took them on the main trail, Astin made a right turn, Sandy knew where she would go, and made the right turn off into the field after her. Sandy then saw her make another turn, with the puppy following. They were quicker, and that was the last Sandy saw of them. She called and called, and finally saw this was useless. After an hour she went back home. Sandy's husband, Joe said, "Astin's here."

Sandy said, "I'm going to kill her, but at least they're back."

Then Joe replied, "They're not back. Astin is back."

By this time it was about 11:00 a.m. Sandy went out to look for the puppy again. Three hours passed. She had not found the puppy. It was winter, very cold, and he was not used to the cold or being outside. Sandy panicked. She took Astin, and rounded up quite a few other people with herding dogs, and retrievers, to help her look. Still no puppy. It was now nighttime. Staying up all night, calling this dog that didn't even know his name, she barked, howled and pleaded. She thought he might be scared into barking. There was only silence.

The woods were endless. Sandy kept looking with other dogs. When one got tired, she would go back and get a different one. She had experiences with dogs becoming feral after just a few hours of being lost. They become frightened and disoriented; they don't appear to know you. She thought he would relate better to another dog, so she just kept searching with them. She had visions of the puppy starving and becoming weaker. At least there was plenty of water, as it was raining.

Sandy called me on a Tuesday night. She had exhausted every other possibility. Then she remembered that a friend of hers knew someone with psychic abilities who had found a lost dog in New York City, after the dog had been gone for about six weeks. She called her friend, and was given my name and phone number. Exhausted and panicked she was barely able to get the words out. All I heard was that a puppy was missing.

"Sandy, please don't say anything else. Let me tell you what I can first. You can let me know if I'm making any sense. I see a garage and willow trees."

She said, "Willow trees don't grow wild, and I've been all through the woods, hundreds and hundreds of acres. There are only two willow trees and I planted them myself by my barn, which is 500 feet from the house."

I continued: "I also see sewers, pipes and ditches."

She answered, "There ain't no such thing."

"And a golf course."

"Wrong," she said. "You're completely off base."

Then I told her to let me think about this overnight and that I would get back to her in the morning. Sandy felt as though her last hope had vanished into thin air. After we hung up Sandy started thinking. There were no sewers, but the power company came into these woods not that long ago, maybe ten years ago. They wanted to put up power lines. There was a river and they couldn't put up the lines. They came also to build a road, and what did they do? They brought these great big sewer pipes and threw them in what Sandy thought was a tributary of a river. They thought they could cover them with dirt, and drive their trucks over them. Then Sandy said to herself, "sewer pipes." She also realized that I had said ditches. Sandy went off to question one of her neighbors. Sandy's neighbor, who lives in an old farmhouse (this land was part of a farmstead about 100 years ago) filled her in. When this was a farm, lots of times it went under water, so they had to dig ditches. They dug at least twenty of them. These ditches were dug from the high part to the low part. Then they built a big ditch that went into the river. They are sewer pipes now." What Sandy thought was a river was really a drainage ditch. Now, it's the middle of the night, it's pouring, and out she went, to search around the ditches about a half mile from her house. Altogether she found four sewage drainage pipes.

Sandy was afraid the dog had drowned, so down she went, crawling through this ditch. Remember that it was just water, not a sewer. No dog. She went home, but as soon as the sun came up she went out again. She started following some side tributaries, and followed them up towards the house, where they disappeared. They had been covered up for over 100 years. She found them all. Then she looked for a golf course, found none, then thought, "Wait a minute. The main ditch goes out to the Pastiche River. Now where this ends and all these little drainage ditches come down to it, across the river is a defunct golf course. They built a golf course and it went under water. There is a fairway right across the river."

Sandy ran home to call me and tell me what she had found.

I told Sandy, "The dog isn't far away. You are confusing him. Remember, dogs don't think in English. They understand intonations. They can picture. If you believe in all the electrical impulses that bring birds home and dogs back, what you are doing is confusing to the dog. You're hysterical. There is this little thing out there, frightened, and if you are mentally sending anything, you are sending terribly frightening things. Clear your mind, concentrate on bringing him home. The things I keep seeing are the barn, willow trees, and garage. Bring the dog back."

Sandy sat for hours, and when she went out she would also visualize the little dog and imagine bringing him to these trails. Once he found the main trail that led to her house, he couldn't get lost. Now it's Wednesday. Sandy called me.

My only comment was: "I don't see death. He's very quiet, and he's very near."

Now it's nearly a week later and it's hunting season. Sandy asked any hunters she saw to please watch out for the dog and to try to bring him home. She called me again and I asked her to come to my house and bring me something the dog had slept on. Her husband, Joe drove her to my house. By this time she was nearly suicidal. She had no hope, she couldn't tell Donald. She was really at the end. She brought some little dog toys.

I looked at her and said, "You have to go on with your life."

I turned to Joe and said to him, "If you don't get her some help, I will. She's in very bad shape."

This was a nightmare for Sandy. I told Sandy the dog would show up on Sunday. I told her to stop looking for him, he would just show up. Joe promised he would get her to a therapist and they left. When they arrived home, Sandy called the dog breeder (not Donald) whom they had bought the puppy from and told her the entire story. The breeder said she had another dog.

"We won't tell Donald," Sandy and the breeder agreed.

These puppies were identical. Maybe they would wait six months and then tell him, or maybe never tell him. She questioned how the breeder could sell her another dog, when she had just lost one. The breeder said it was an accident, and she knew she didn't do it on purpose.

She said, "I'd like to tell you a story about accidents. You've known me about 18 years, but 23 years ago I had a little boy. My husband and I were going to a dinner, and I let my sister and brother-in-law take my little boy for the night. He was two years old. In the morning my brother-in-law went for a walk with his German shepherd and my son. They lived near a park with a lake. They were walking in the park on a cold winter morning. He heard a sound and turned around, and the child was gone. He had fallen into the lake, under the ice. He died. Don't tell me about accidents. It wasn't anyone's fault, yet they are still blaming themselves for it."

Then the breeder let Sandy have the dog. Now it was Sunday, and Joe was afraid to leave her alone, she was so distraught. At 8:30 a.m., Joe asked her if she would mind staying alone for a few minutes, so he could go out to get a newspaper. She said she was not fine, but pulling herself together a bit more, she thought it would be OK. He came back about 15 minutes later. He's a very laid-back person, with a quiet, gentle, and easygoing manner.

As he entered the house, his voice was raised as he spoke to Sandy, "What the hell did you do?"

Sandy did not understand, and asked what the matter was.

He replied, "I don't understand you. I don't believe you're this stupid. You lose a dog, we have spent the last seven days in total torture. Now, we get the other dog, we won't talk about what you had to pay for him, so why would you let the new dog outside alone?"

Sandy said, "I didn't let him out."

Joe kept yelling, "Why did you let the new puppy out?"

Sandy asked, "Out where? Where is he?"

Joe answered, "Out in the garage. I drove into the garage and almost hit him. He was sitting there."

Sandy was confused, but knew there was no way the puppy could have gotten out. They went to the garage and the puppy was still sitting there.

Sandy, now totally confused, said, "Where is his ear tape? I just did his ears. My God, he's thin."

She stared at him and said, "Wait a minute. I think the new puppy is still in the house, asleep. Let me check." Sandy ran into the house and yelled, "Puppy's in here."

Joe then asked, "Well then what is this sitting in here? What do you mean he's in there? He's in here. I'm looking right at him."

Sandy ran back into the garage with the second puppy and said, "Here he is."

Joe asked, "Then what's this? This is weird, it's exactly seven days to the hour that the first puppy was lost. Now we have two puppies, one very thin!"

Sandy ran into the house to call me. Then she called Donald. Two weeks later, she drove both puppies to Donald's house in Maryland so he could choose one. They were identical except the lost puppy had a totally different personality from the week before he was lost. He had become assertive, even with the other puppy. The other puppy had been the dominant one in the pack. Donald took the first puppy for a year and showed him. The dog was doing really well. Donald died and his widow was left with the dog. Sandy spoke to her every day, and she told her one day that something was wrong with the dog and she didn't know what it was. The dog was getting stranger every day. This was an 80-pound full-grown doberman.

Sandy went to Maryland to pick up the dog, because he was having separation anxiety. He would rip up the room every time Donald's widow left. Sandy and Joe had to keep this dog and his brother separated.

Sandy told me, "He is definitely strange. When he is upset, he whirls and whirls. Astin, the infamous surrogate mother, died. Now if the dog needs to go out and it's raining, he howls and cries and shivers."

Two years later, I was the featured speaker at a kennel club. I spoke to a room full of people about my animal stories. I recognized Sandy and Joe in the audience. After my lecture, Sandy stood up. She asked if I ever get to meet the people or the animals that I have found.

"Very rarely," I said.

Smiling, Sandy said, "Well, I have a treat for you."

Joe brought the Doberman out, a big, friendly dog. He turned him loose. He walked right to me, though we had never met, and stopped dead in his tracks. He looked at me. I patted him. He walked away to visit some other people. I sat on the floor, and then the dog just stopped, as if something had happened. He whirled around, all four feet at once, then ran back over to me, climbed into my lap, put his head on my shoulder, and closed his eyes. Now, in dog language, this is total submissive behavior.

"He has never done this with anyone before," Sandy commented.

I don't know exactly how the dog knew me, but he knew me. It was a complete submission to a mother, according to Sandy. She and I spoke years later. She shared that he had never done this with anyone else since. Having had that experience a few times before, convinced me that there is a communication that occurs when love is the sole energy that connects one to the other.

In 1976, Adele, who had been transcribing what came through me when I was in deep trance, called one night to ask for my help with her dog. When quieting my thoughts, and focusing on the idea of a flow between the dog and me as best friends, I received some ideas of where the difficulties were. I relayed them to Adele. Adele called back a few days later to thank me. She invited me to her home. I pulled up, and got out of the car. A ten-pound furball came flying down the few steps outside the house and flung himself into my arms. That, according to Adele, was not something he ever did before.

Once we consider that teachers come in all sizes, shapes, and species we can experience the natural power of creation within all life. Think of all the friends that get us through tough times, and how a friendly tone, a kind touch, compassionate listening, can soothe us. If we apply the same to all species, we witness how they love and appreciate the same loving qualities.

They don't care if they know our language, they know the universal language of love.

*Petting, scratching, and cuddling a dog could be as soothing to
the mind and heart as deep meditation and almost as good for
the soul as prayer.* —Dean Koontz

Iris Nevins and I became friends after she had a reading with me in 1987. Besides her incredible ability as an artist who helped resurrect the art of marbleized paper, and so much more, she tells of the time when she had a pack of five shelties. They lived a life of canine luxury on her New Jersey farm. She recounted the following to me.

"They have three different fenced-in yards, totaling about five acres, where they can run and have adventures to their hearts content. They also have a small old barn for shelter, which is divided into two rooms. It may well be the largest 'dog house' in the whole state. When the sun goes down, the dogs come into the main house, where they spend the evening with the family, sharing tidbits of our dinner (they are terribly spoiled!) . They fall asleep wherever they like. The three males are very protective, and sleep in the bedroom at night to keep watch over us.

"My friend, Leslie, was dog-sitting for her friend Janet's sheltie, Sheba. I remember it was a Tuesday, August 23, 1994, when I got a call from Leslie. She had to go out of town, and needed someone to watch Sheba and her own dog, Tanner. I am a dog person and consider Tanner one of my best friends. I even taught him how to talk. Whenever I would visit, Tanner would hear my car, come running up to me howling, 'I wuw woo, I wuw woo!' Then I would calm him down, and tell him that I loved him, to which he would reply, 'I wuw woo woo.' I knew he loved me too. I wished I could take him, but unfortunately my three males did not like other males visiting, but I did say I would take Sheba, an adorable little female. I thought she would have a lot of fun with my new little puppy, Juniper.

"I had met Sheba a few times before. She was a nervous dog, and when Leslie brought her over she was a bit frightened by my howling pack of dogs. They were all very curious, and it was apparent that Sheba was not enjoying having five other Shelties sniffing at her. Leslie drove off as I took Sheba inside the house to give her some leftover meat. She decided I was OK and followed me.

"I put Sheba in a separate yard with my two female shelties. I watched the three female dogs for the next hour, bringing more meat out to them several times, making sure Sheba was OK. I felt sure everything was fine. I went out for the afternoon. I knew the dogs couldn't get out of the fence. I drove my car down the driveway, and Sheba ran after me along the fence. I got out at the end of the drive and reassured her I would be back in a few hours. She seemed upset that I was leaving, but I thought she would calm down after I left.

"When I came back later that afternoon, Sheba was gone. We searched all over the huge yard, behind trees and bushes, and only found one little spot under the fence where she could have possibly tunneled under. She may also have climbed the fence. We will never know for sure how she got out. I called every police station, veterinarian, shelter, and animal control person in our county and surrounding ones. Sheba's owner was off hiking in the woods in Maine and we could not reach her, so I left a message on her answering machine in Pennsylvania, hoping she might call home for her messages. I even called three radio stations in the area, and had them make announcements several times a day.

"I called Nancy, who said she thought Sheba dug her way out of the fence and was heading home. The poor dog must have been so frightened and confused. I was exhausted from driving all around looking for the dog.

"Nancy said, 'I see that someone will pick her up in two days, and bring her back to your house. Right now I see her at an abandoned railroad bed.'

"I thanked her, but could not sit around and wait for someone to return Sheba. I went to the only abandoned railroad bed I knew of in the area and started to holler "Sheba." Now it was Tuesday night. We took Buster, our smartest male, out looking for Sheba. If she was around, Buster would find her. It was getting dark. There was no sign of Sheba anywhere. I stopped people on bicycles to ask them, but no one had seen her. She was a shy dog, and I was afraid she would stay well-hidden from anyone who was not familiar.

"The next two days were spent looking. It was not until late Wednesday night that I heard from Janet, Sheba's owner. She was very understanding, and told me not to blame myself. She said she would drive from Maine the next morning and help look for Sheba. I called Nancy a few more times. She thought Sheba was pretty close by. I thought, if she was hiding somewhere on the farm, which has quite a lot of acreage, she might come out if she heard her master's voice.

"When Janet arrived Thursday afternoon at about three o'clock, I was a mess. I had hardly eaten or slept since Tuesday. It's bad enough when you lose your own dog, but it's so much worse when it belongs to someone else. Janet called all through the fields and woods; still no Sheba. We decided to get in the car, and drive to Leslie's house to see if she made her way back there. As we drove, I told Janet about Nancy, and how good she was at finding missing animals. She hoped Nancy was right. Nancy had told me to mentally tell Sheba to go to a place where people could see her, so she could be picked up and brought back.

"A few hours later we were still driving around. We decided we would go to see Nancy with one of Sheba's toys that evening, if we didn't find her. We were somehow fairly confident that we would find Sheba. I have kept a phone in my car for the past year or so for emergency use. I use it so infrequently, that I was startled when I heard something ringing softly. Janet and I both said, 'What's that?' I realized it was the phone. I felt so silly, I didn't even know which button answered the phone for a few seconds.

When I answered, my daughter was saying, 'A trooper just brought Sheba home!' I asked her if she was sure it was Sheba, and not another sheltie. She said she was sure. We called Nancy and told her, as we headed back to the farm.

"When we got there, Sheba was there, a complete mess, full of burrs. As it turned out, a trooper from our local police barracks, the first person I spoke to, was the one to find her. She was picked up about three miles from my house in a small town. The trooper saw a dog that looked like a fox, and remembered my description. She wouldn't come to him when he called her name, so he parked his car, opened the back door and sat down in the driver's seat. A minute later, Sheba, who is very used to riding in cars, jumped right in. Nancy was right again. Just two days later and someone did pick the dog up, and bring her back, just as she had seen."

It's always struck me as odd that each of these moments of tuning in, I can still replay in detail in my mind. I think it's an equation of sorts, a recipe that combines a physiological happening, a pineal gland (we all have a third eye, the pineal gland is loaded with optical receptors just like our two eyes), a desire to be of service, and an ability to capture a thought as it passes by in milliseconds. Maybe it starts with my love of puzzles, games, and a psychological need to resolve and alleviate pain. When teaching or being interviewed, I love talking about the pineal gland and brain forming an equation of light and dark, creating images received from our Creator, to our Soul, and then to our self. Now when that happens, I literally see it forming inside me. Is it real? Is talking with a deceased dog real? How do we know? For me it is the feedback. If I know that the dog you love who is on the other side, remembers fondly the stuffed rabbit it played with, who is sending that idea to me? It can take days, weeks, or months before the answer comes. When it does, and I'm correct, it reassures me that all life, when leaving behind their form, moves on to the next journey.

There is no death, only a change of worlds. —Chief Seattle

Think of when you can't find your…keys, phone, anything. The person who looks and looks generally speaking won't find it, or the dog, cat, horse, etc. Pressure stops the flow from one to another, even with inanimate objects. That's why a police officer may be concerned yet keeps his/her cool. We can all make a difference if we help the person most frustrated by losing someone. We can serve as a loving anchor. We may not have all the answers, but what we do have, is the ability to enter into the situation with no pressure, only the desire to be of service. Sometimes it leads others to carry on the work. Robin is one of those people.

Robin sent me an email telling her story. Robin's four-year-old toy poodle Taco ran away. A nervous, easily scared dog, he usually clung to her. Robin and her husband were going through a divorce, which she felt confused Taco. With the help of family and friends, they searched for hours.

Robin said: "At night, I would cry knowing Taco was alone, wondering if he had shelter and food, hoping my love for him would protect and keep him safe. By day two, all our efforts had failed, and a good friend suggested I call Nancy. She might have the wisdom, guidance and insight that we needed to find him.

"The rangers at a park three miles from where we lived, saw him once a day. When they approached him, he ran. I was talking to Nancy, and she assured me that when domestic animals go on an adventure, most have the ability to adjust to the wilderness. She went on to explain, Taco would be capable of finding scraps of food and shelter. A lost dog typically moves in a large circle spiraling in towards home or wherever they are hoping is home.

"They can roam around in circles for several days. She suggested I place a familiar toy and a piece of clothing along the path where he was spotted. I felt comforted after talking to her, and thought there was a real chance of finding Taco.

"Knowing all this, we decided to leave a truck that Taco spent a lot of time in, at the park, overnight with the door open. The morning of day five, we found Taco sleeping on the seat of the old truck. This was one of the happiest mornings of my life.

"Two years past, and I was running with my girlfriend, when a woman in her car stopped to ask if we had seen her lost dog, Emily, a golden retriever. I tried to help the woman with the information I had learned from Nancy. She was too upset to listen. My friend and I decided we would extend our experience finding Taco, to trying to find Emily. We could be more logical in our effort, without the anxiety of the lost dog belonging to us. Within three days, we found Emily, persuaded her to come to us with a piece of cheese, and collared her. The people who missed her, loved her, and needed her in their life had her back.

"And the beat goes on,

"Robin"

Until we extend our circle of compassion to all living things, humanity will not find peace. —Albert Schweitzer

Opening the doors to help, always helps me come out of my shell. Loving to offer whatever I can, I've learned that each time is different, each time teaches me about something I wasn't aware of before. The aha's are endless, and they become my proof that all life is connected. Getting feedback is the only way I know that my intention to channel a message for the highest good, is useful. Here is an email I received that helped me know that the time we spent together was helpful:

Also, I want to thank you for the session that you did this past April 3rd with my dog Natasha and myself. Before the session, I felt that the end of her life was near, and I was seeking help in saying goodbye to her. During the session, you communicated to me from her, that she was NOT ready to go, yet. After the session, she really "came back to life" (ironically on the day before Easter!!) and we have had (and continue to have) a richer, deeper connection than ever before. And she wasn't the only one that changed!! She continues to suffer from the crippling degenerative myelopathy; she has good times and bad times, and is progressively but slowly, losing her physical abilities. I have learned so much about how to care for her physically, AND nurture her spirit (and let her nurture mine). I greatly appreciate what you did for us. Some time ago, I saw flyers for a workshop that you were offering around communicating with animals. Are you planning to offer it or something similar in the near future?

If you have men who will exclude any of God's creatures from the shelter of compassion and pity, you will have men who will deal likewise with their fellow men.

– Francis of Assisi

Chapter 6

Horses are my Teachers

The 1940's were a time of ponies in Brooklyn. I vaguely remember getting dressed up in a navy blue hat, navy blue and white checkered coat over a navy blue dress, with of course, navy shoes and white socks. I was ready for the big adventure. Next thing I remember, my father stuck me on a pony. The pony was creamy colored, docile, and old. All I remember was having to smile for a picture and being terrified of sitting on this very large beast.

Brooklyn, 1949, on the pony with my sister Anita

That was not only the first time I sat on anything resembling a horse, it was the last, at age nineteen. I worked as a nurse on a medical unit, where a 300-pound woman was admitted under a false diagnosis of congestive heart failure. Her physician readily admitted afterwards that he couldn't find a bed in a nursing home that weekend. Her real diagnosis was advanced dementia. I wheeled her into her room. She stood and launched herself at me, throwing me to the ground. I felt something go snap! That night I drove to the emergency room. That became eleven months out of the next two years in a hospital bed. I was outfitted with a complete body brace for stability. The night before my twenty-first birthday, I was rushed into the operating room. They picked the disc tissue that had completely ruptured off from my sciatic nerve. That began a journey that has been the worst and the best of my life. My *Life of a Psychic Detective* relates how at age twenty-five, and five months pregnant, my first husband attempted to murder us. We, my soon-to-be daughter and I, survived. A year later, I was again rushed in for emergency surgery. Now another disc had been completely destroyed, and the sciatic root on the left side was dying. I was eligible for government assistance for a permanent disability (I rejected the idea) and believed fervently what Helen Keller said: "When one door of happiness closes, another opens; but often we look so long at the closed door that we do not see the one which has been opened for us." I needed to find another door.

Remembering how my parents kept me from continuing the study of ballet, after eleven years of it, because they didn't believe it was the right path for a Jewish girl, I then decided I wanted to be a doctor. That too was dismissed. They refused to pay for the SATs, a requirement for any four-year college. I knew I could enter nursing school at Brooklyn College; it was a two-year program and my grades were the only criteria. They were shocked. That pleased me. My family bet I would drop out, since it was no career for a girl, who they thought should simply get married. That choice propelled me to be the best version of myself. I took a deep dive into learning to be a nurse, and found that I loved helping others. It became a path that lifted my spirit by caring for others. I can still remember every job I had as a nurse. I've always hoped that Florence Nightingale would have been proud of me.

After several years of working while in pain, a door I had been hoping for showed itself. An experimental ten-day stay, twelve-bed acute psychiatric unit was being created in the old Lincoln Hospital in the South Bronx. After going on interviews, and turning down jobs in psychiatric hospitals, because I believed their choices of treatment were archaic, this one was amazing for me. It allowed me to do what I love best, using my gifts to help others.

When I left, it was a difficult decision. I knew I needed to stay home even though financially it looked impossible. My body was suffering from the hours of driving, working, and caring for my precious daughter. Inside, I was screaming in pain; outside, I was tight as a drum. Believing no one needed to hear my sob story, I felt I was completely alone. Married to someone who, as my second husband, began to treat my daughter as an outsider broke my heart. It also angered me to have blindly believed that he would love her because she was a child. He seemed to in the first year, but then any difficulty she had in adjusting was treated as unfair to him. I married a child. The line "It takes a village to raise a child" is one I've always believed would be the way the world would be a far safer place.

It was a relief to be home with my daughter instead of seeing her when I was exhausted. We had just moved to a small converted barn with two bedrooms and one bathroom, in Peekskill, New York. Shortly after I became pregnant. This was when he still knew to show love to his step-daughter.

When I was nine months pregnant, my husband lost his job. We were now on his unemployment insurance, with no savings. Three of my friends and I formed an organic food coop. It was a great move, since it became cheaper than buying any food in a supermarket. In one year we had 500 members!

After giving birth, I realized my spinal issues were not going away, and the pain was nonstop. With no income coming in from either of us, I started deep breathing and relating to all of life as the necessary connection to sustain mine. I would soon find myself in a very different view of the world.

At age 31, desperate for help, I attended the first psychic reading of my life. It was set up by my second husband, and I reluctantly went. Irwin Grief worked from home. His family had just finished dinner, when he took me to another room, set up a tape recorder, and jumped into a past life reading before I could even grasp the concept.

"You were a young woman, or teenager, when you fell off your pony and permanently injured your spine. That is why you have spinal deformities in this life; you carried them forward."

Although I scoffed at his statement, and dismissed it, I couldn't shake my curiosity at how he knew about my spinal deformities. Two years prior, I received a call from one of the inventors of the spinal tomogram, Dr. Robert E. Jacobson. This would give them the ability to have a 3D view of my spine. He had been in the same neurosurgical residency program at Albert Einstein as my first husband. He knew my injuries, as did the Chief of Neurosurgery, Dr. Hubert Rosomoff. They wanted to take a look. They were wonderfully kind and honest. All I needed to do was get myself to the hospital in Florida where they could take the film.

The view showed something I never knew before. I was born with a rare condition, no disc between lumbar 5 and sacral 1, severe spinal stenosis, and bone spurs throughout the base of the spine, which led to a condition that left my body paralyzed sometimes, spondylolisthesis. How did Irwin Grief know I was born that way?

During the last 45 years finding missing animals, including one precious Chincoteague pony, healing work with horses, explaining to owners/trainers what their horse was saying, I'd been offered lots of lessons. My spine was so unstable I turned down the offers. Each time I have been with a horse or pony I feel like I am with an old friend.

Having moved to New Jersey, divorced again, and working full time as a psychic, I was on a completely new path. I became far less stressed, loved giving psychic readings, and jumped into new ideas like why not read a pet? If I could talk to the other side, why not talk with a deceased pet? I needed to love all living, and those gone onto their next adventure.

All of this led to being able to talk to pet owners not only through tuning in. I have been concerned about the amount of toxins in their food, shampoos, and so much more. Because I believe everything is connected, I became a volunteer joining the late Dr. Wally Burnstein's activist group seeking to ban food irradiation plants in New Jersey. Then I met folk singer Elaine Silver during yoga classes. We became friends, and when she was bored with her songs, we wrote twelve songs together. My life was incredibly different. I felt more fulfilled and ready to explore, and discover more of my soul. I was waking up.

One man attended both Wally's meeting for volunteers and Elaine Silver's public singing. That's how I met the love of my life, Dick Weber.

Having been involved in past life regression therapy since the 1970s, I keep thinking that we don't have all the answers. When my husband, the Dickens as I love to call him, left a message for me one day, it would lead me to consider something that was surprised me, it was did I live before?

Dick was attending a military surplus auction. His first of two he would attend: one for him, and one for my revenge. I was working the morning he left for the first auction.

His voice message left me perplexed. "Sweetheart, you are the proud owner of 128 used bowling pins! And all for $21. Can't wait to see you."

It wasn't as if he didn't have enough in our dungeon. The dungeon was my nickname for the basement that cries for itself. I swear I heard it pleading, fix me, clean me. If I can hear birds, I certainly can hear the consciousness of my own home. I did hear it, and it is now a beautiful 1,000 square feet of relaxation that I call my spa home.

The Dickens came home. Yes, the bowling pins were ridiculous, and yes, they stayed far too long. Almost a year later, with the help of a friend Lee, the little critters were transformed into perfect pre-bunny forms for kindergartners throughout northern New Jersey. To all the parents who received these as gifts, I hope you enjoyed your child's creative use of Dickens' extravaganza.

Now about my revenge and how a pony is involved. Many months later, my body started tripping me up. I accepted the temporary help of a wheelchair. Sitting near the stove, pouring boiling water into my waiting coffee press of vanilla, organic, freshly ground coffee, one cup a day treat, the silly arm and hand attached to the teapot weakened and boiling water cascaded down the front of my opened robe. Of course I had no clothes on—great for total coverage of third-degree burns. Self-treating quickly and repeatedly, I have no scars; however, the ensuing days were difficult. During that time, Dick did not know what to do for me. Here was his dancing Nancy in a wheelchair with the upper part of her body crispy.

He came up with, "Would you like to go to a military auction? You've always wanted to see one."

If you've never been to one, picture a dirty, all gray in every respect, humongous warehouse about 25,000 square feet with long wooden tables going down half the length of the building. He wheeled me between these rows of tables. Every so often, a paper with a number was tacked near a grouping of stuff. These were the pallets that would be bid on. They supposedly corresponded to the information on the papers they handed out. Once bidding began, these rows were roped off. When a bid was accepted, you had to buy it if you ever wanted to come back. That's how Dick inadvertently bought bowling pins instead of some computer supplies. Wrong number.

A simple thought can lead to lots of work, like "these books are fascinating." Eighty-four dollars later, I thought I was the proud owner of a pallet of books I looked at. Nope, it was 1,500 pounds of the West Point Army Library used book collection, all of it. It was the entire row! Our recycling center was kept busy, along with all our friends who walked away from our garage, nicknamed West Point #2, with armloads of books. Summer came and we still had a garage filled with them. Dick was outside by the open garage door, ripping covers off books to go to the recycling center. At the time our home-based office had a fax machine. Both of us are also ministers, so when a wedding couple faxed me the poem "How Do I Love Thee?" by Elizabeth Barrett Browning, I brought it out to show Dick. I love that poem and wanted to share with him how happy I was to be able to say this one at a wedding. Before I could speak he said:

"Nancy, do you remember the poem "How Do I Love Thee?" I've got to say it at a wedding this week-end and I'd like your interpretation of the rhythm, and feel of it."

"I love it! And the couple I'm working with sent it as their choice too! The woman wrote that she is a cousin of Elizabeth Barrett, her last name being Barrett. Isn't it strange, both of us get to say it miles apart on the same day?"

The next day a friend, LeeAnn, arrived with her 13-year-old daughter Amy. LeeAnn and I plopped two lawn chairs in front of the garage and continued the process of preparing the books for recycling. It was time to get rid of all the now-moldy books that had served their purpose. Amy wanted to start in the back of the garage by the wet, moldy papers. Warning her to be careful and not stay there too long, Lee and I settled back to talk and scan the collection.

"Oh! Elizabeth Barrett Browning."

"Amy, what about her?"

"I'll show you."

Among the hundreds of ruined books in the dark and wet garage, Amy found something to do with the author of "How Do I Love Thee?" She handed me a dark blue hard-cover book. The spine stated "*Mrs. Browning's*

Complete Poetical Words, Cambridge Edition, Houghton Mifflin Co." The front cover has a gold wreath encircling "Elizabeth Barrett Browning." It was the first edition and signed by her niece. On the first page, a signature states "Erica Clarkson Barrett, Philadelphia, Dec. 13, 1914."

Opening this remarkable piece of literature, I discovered that it was the only one of my military auction books still in perfect condition. It also looked as if it had never been read. I read that Elizabeth Barrett Browning was a happily physical child until 15 years of age. She rode a pony she loved. One day in an attempt to mount her pony unaided, she fell. This caused serious spinal injuries, which left her an invalid and led to her death in her mid-50s. I started thinking of the weird and only hospitalization I had as a child, at age 15. Nothing ever found, but I lost weight like crazy and was in constant pain. I read further. Elizabeth started her writing at age 31. That was when I entered my new vocation and left my traditional nursing behind. Coincidence or synchronicity? Past life or simply resonance of similar occurrences? I don't have the answer, it just makes me more curious.

Do you believe you have past lives? Remember them? If you are unsure, there is one book I read after my own experiences. I suggest you read *Twenty Cases Suggestive of Reincarnation* by Dr. Ian Stevenson. He was at the University of Virginia School of Medicine for fifty years, chair of the department of psychiatry from 1957 to 1967, Carlson Professor of Psychiatry from 1967 to 2001, and Research Professor of Psychiatry from 2002 until his death.

For me there are no conclusions. What the connection is between that wonderful authoress and myself, I'm not sure. She would appreciate my discomfort at climbing onto the back of a pony or a horse. She would understand my desire to write "thee" and "thou" and speak it when I was about 14, 15, and 16. It felt better than Brooklynese. Whether we knew each other, I was her, or I have access to her energy, her soul, her spirit; something does reach across the boundaries of time and space. Although it is possible to make declarative statements, it seems silly. Answers I glean from my own perspective, through my own filters, ideas, but that does not make it a fact. What if when I die and go on, I discover that it isn't quite the way I thought it was? I make no absolutes and no apology for thinking there are alternative answers. Whether I ever ride a horse or not, whether it is my karma, dharma, or dogma won't even matter. If I enjoy the connections I have with horses, snakes, dogs, and cats, then it will surely balance out any problems I have with horses, snakes, dogs and cats. I have to mention snakes; I am in the process of learning to love what was behind my greatest fears.

Recently I saw a video of a king cobra entwined in fish netting that would kill him. I kept passing up the video, then felt compelled to look at it. A man rescued this king cobra, first offering him enough water to help him through. The trust between both of them was amazing to watch. The understanding of the dangers was not because the snake wanted to hurt him, it was simply a protective device that would be smart to take into account. The man carefully removed the netting that was choking the poor snake. I closed the video and cried in joy when the snake was released from near death. I can empathize when the mask of fear is removed.

All fears of external life forms are illusions. The real fear has been masked by something else, something handy to externalize what is difficult to face. The greatest challenges hold the greatest gifts. I can still feel joy at the snake's release. I am so happy for him, even though I think of him as a danger for many.

The object of the fear is a manifested mirror. Having family members terrified of other living beings actually helped clarify the truth. It couldn't possibly be the spider's fault. No one in my family had suffered at the hands of an insect, cat, dog, or other being, at least not in this lifetime. These bugs and animals did not create the problem. Because it was so obvious, it actually served to guide me in my search for understanding.

Today, after years of changes, therapy, meditation, injuries, near deaths, being raped, and births and deaths of loved ones, the tenuous thread is now a strong and loving rope that guides me. Having had a snake phobia, I know that all the hatred, prejudices, and fears are simply the negative portion of my own personal mind, not about anyone or anything else.

Gathering the best of our thoughts, the sweetest and kindest of our beliefs and manifesting them, guarantees us a moment-to-moment joy that no fear or hatred can supersede. I believe that is why the poorest of the poor can have a smile that melts an iceberg. Spirit is fully present, and I have seen this joyful manner in Herman the fly, Baby the groundhog, and Dick the husband.

I remember having to drive an hour and a half and felt lonely when I stepped into my car. A fly followed me in, and proceeded to sit on the steering wheel, seemingly staring at me. I stared back, and the name Herman popped up. He sat there for the whole drive and flew away when I opened the door. Days later, I was at a gathering outdoors. Someone was about to swat a fly when he landed on the edge of my cup. I stopped them, and looked at the fly telling him about Herman (with my inside voice). He bopped me on the nose, then sat on the edge of the cup again. I could swear he was laughing. Yes, my friends all wondered what happened to my mind. That is, until they needed my help. Their excitement at being more than they thought they were, would be the beginning of their new journey.

There is a divine presence operating the life force within every being. Approaching each sentient being with a consciously open heart and mind with offerings of joyful love creates a bridge with the trees, flowers, birds, insects, reptiles, mammals, and most of all, the soul of life itself.

Imagine your personal mind is one track, with an overlapping universal mind track that is not just connected to all else, it is all else. When we acknowledge that, we are asking for the universal mind to vibrate at its highest divine resonance for our conscious connection with other life forms. Soul to Soul, we can then observe the depth of the interaction, letting go of the labels, the skunk, rabbit, parrot, etc. We are now able to pass through the surface into the oneness. The moments where we feel love of life, not just ours or our family's, we feel the Creator creating the tapestry of life itself. We can then ask the questions we would ask our best friend, our soul mate, our children, our pets. Ask as if they are our closest kin, for in that moment they are.

In 1976, when I was short and young—just kidding, I was never short but I was younger—I was walking towards an exit in Grand Central Station in New York City, and as I was about to pass the information booth, a voice screamed out, "Oh my God, I've been bitten." Turning around, I saw a young woman, normally probably pale, go absolutely gray with eyes stuttering in fear. I walked over and she immediately lifted her T-shirt a few inches to show me her very swollen, rapidly reddening and spreading bite by something on her abdomen. I took her by the hand with, "Come with me; I'm a nurse." I was shocked at what I said. That was the first and last time I used my license to convince someone to trust me.

Taking her hand, I led her to the ladies room. Like magic, a chair was there waiting for her. As she sat down, I let the power of the urge to heal guide my movements, words, and actions. My hands on her head and hers over her abdomen, I instructed her to breathe in cool, pale blues and greens to the area. Not more than five minutes went by when she opened her eyes and looked down remarking that it no longer hurt. We both saw the area; it was as though nothing was ever there. We held hands walking out to the information booth, where two police officers were waiting to talk with her.

"Thanks, but I no longer need help. She healed it; she's a nurse."

For me, the amazing piece was her trust in the process and her easy acceptance of what to me was a small miracle. I did not heal her. I calmed her so she could let the natural process of self-healing take effect. That led me to believe that it would be easiest to work with the innocent, our pets and wildlife.

That moment led to a quantum leap in risk-taking. Blurting out "I'm a nurse" was one thing. An article appeared in a local newspaper, "Psychic communicates with animals." Reading it, one caller, Linda, spoke.

"I read an article about your work with animals. I have a horse that I need help with; would you please come see him?"

"Sure. What day?"

It didn't matter that the last and only horse I had been near was actually not a horse; it was the pony in Brooklyn. That's the crazy, risky part of me. Go for the deep dive, that's where either the fun or hell reside. I've seen both, and although I've seen the shock on others when I describe some of the wildest deep dives I've taken, I would do it again. I have learned some caution. I'm convinced the Creator, the Source, when fully alight in my being, fuses my soul to myself and provides the best long-term results, for growing me into a decent human being. Armor has come off again and again. The fury at being harmed by other human beings, has led to an intense need to relieve suffering of others regardless of whether they appreciate who I am or not. The soul can whisper and I get clarity. I can shout and the soul laughs at my fears. Calm before and now even during my stormy moments prevails. Connecting the dots between my little-me hurts and my soul has alleviated the thunderstorms that would lay in wait, and then burst out at anyone who blamed me for their own mistakes.

The following Monday I drove west on Route 46. Linda lived in God's Country, acres of flat land, flowers by the side of the road, horses grazing everywhere. Looking past the barns and homes, the land rose like a tidal wave, covered with froth made of trees and stone. The mountains were red and gold, with touches of green.

A woman who looked graceful as a gazelle, with long, straight, light-brown hair, was standing in the driveway. She had stepped out of a back door, when my car pulled up. Linda had a grace about her as if she were flying free across the land.

"Nancy?"

"Hi Linda."

"Would you mind if another person watched besides me?"

"Not at all. Remember, I don't want to know anything about the horse, except perhaps its name. I like to call everybody by their name."

"Amir."

"Thanks."

We walked into the barn. A horse called out. Linda walked over to a stall. "Amir, this is the lady I called to help."

Her hand was stroking his face. Linda put a rope on him with a very short lead.

"Would you mind leading him out to the field? I have to meet Robert, the journalist."

Not bothering to tell Linda I had never been near a horse, I said, "Sure" as I took the lead and started chatting with Amir.

"Hi Amir, come on sweetie; let's go to the beautiful fields."

We stood in the middle of a field scattered with bright floral colors. Never having learned the names of most flowers, all I could spot were the daisies. The blue flowers were like stars that dropped from the sky; pink ones looked like delicate air-brushed fluff and yellow ones looked like pieces of the sun's rays. It was beautiful and helped me center my mind on Amir.

Nancy, Amir and Linda 1979

Connecting with him was easy. I soon found a feeling that translated as a history of trauma. My body seemed to change into a horse's, except that I was the only one who knew that. My front shoulder ached; my head had old damage from a fall as a baby. I could see me as a young colt falling backwards. Then, the image changed to one where all my insides grew sluggish and tired. I knew that feeling well; I labeled that one allergies and stress.

Translating my experience to Linda and Robert was easy. I simply deleted the part where I became an animal. We kinetically muscle tested Amir for feed he ingested. I used Linda as a proxy. Two products seemed to show a weakening in the system. Linda decided to switch to another feed and see if that would help.

"I want us to win in the shows. I know he is good enough."

"Linda, he gets nervous when he doesn't know what's coming. Not unlike many of us, he handles change poorly. If you can go to the place where the show is being held beforehand, and firmly fix an image of it in your mind, it would help. Take that image and stand before him, imagine making mental contact, third eye to third eye, and send the image again and again along an imaginary beam."

At the conclusion, Linda again handed me the rope. Casually, I took it and pulled Amir along. When he resisted, I tugged, laughing, I told Amir he was as stubborn as any man I'd ever met. I kept on pulling and teasing until I turned the rope back to Linda and started to breathe again.

Glad that he was fun and I could handle him, I said, "He was an absolute joy to work with."

"Yes, he was quite different today, thank God. Usually, he kicks and bites. That was one of the reasons I called you. Funny how good he was; you sure do know horses."

Back in the comfort of my car, my mind shook harder than my body at the risk I had just taken. Sometimes I get in trouble and sometimes I don't, but I always like to jump into the world while it's spinning. Linda called a month later to tell me she did everything I showed her and they won their first prize easily. In the years that followed they consistently won and grew very close as friends.

Linda invited me to her wedding two years later. When she and her husband separated, she came to live in my home in Budd Lake. Amir was moved to a friend's farm. Six months later, Linda was ready to move to her own place.

A few years later, Linda attended my wedding on February 11, 1989. A month later, her sister called to tell me that Linda went mountain climbing for the first time. (She went with her boyfriend, an avid climber, and his friend, an expert teacher.) Linda fell off the mountain and died. I know Linda is handling her world better than her family and friends are handling missing her. As much as I understand and believe in life after life and reincarnation, it doesn't make the loss go away. It does add other ingredients: comfort to know she's okay, mysterious meetings out of body, her voice ringing true and clear in my mind. All these stretch the emotions into acceptance. Linda knows that she helped me start a journey that has led me to meet many other horses and ponies who, like Amir, could use some extra heaping of loving help.

A great horse will change your life. The truly special ones define it. —Author unknown

My precious friend Phyllis's husband Kenny, and his partner Louis, bought racehorses. One day while visiting Phyllis, Kenny mentioned one of his horses.

"His lungs need to be looked at." Kenny was used to me blurting out odd comments.

As he responded with "he's fine," the phone rang. Unbeknown to Kenny, that very morning, a groom noticed the horse had a breathing problem and called for a vet. The vet reported he found an issue in his lungs. Weeks later, Kenny asked me to go with him to the stable where he wanted me to evaluate four horses. Kenny and some friends were their owners. Like most racehorses, they were being trained by experts who also were their keepers. The trainer, along with that year's top racing jockey, were present. The jockey watched with open amusement as I saw the energy of each horse and spoke of their needs. When he learned that I was not a vet, nor had I ever been there before, he couldn't figure out how I knew since he could confirm most of what I saw. His puzzled expression turned to annoyance. He was determined to unmask me as a charlatan, and he showed it. The internal rebel in me was rising, a trigger that would get my stubborn and willful side stronger by the minute. My mother took me to racetracks when I was ten. Once she had me wait outside the gate, since I was too young to be let in. She would ask me what number to bet on. Every race, I picked a winner. It was the only time she liked my gifts. It took a few years to recognize how terrified she was of the ability to know beyond the usual, except for gambling. Here was her attitude in the form of an arrogant guy. Only his fear later turned into genuine appreciation.

The jockey asked to show me another horse and took me to the stall. Standing outside the stall, only seeing the horse's head, I stated, "The horse goes lame in the front left leg on an inside curve, compensation problems probably."

"Wrong, it's the right leg."

After a few back and forths, I asked if someone could walk the horse around the curve. The front left leg began buckling as soon as they walked around a curve. The jockey was visibly disturbed. Goodie.

"One more horse, just this one more."

Now I stood in front of a stall of another horse letting several minutes pass.

"How am I supposed to tell you anything? I don't speak French, and this horse does not know English; it's from France."

"My god, how do you know the horse is from France?"

"She told me."

Of course, if I didn't understand French how could she have told me? He reminded me of the man who had burglarized my home two years prior. I saw him putting my then-husband's (husband #2) rifle (which I was glad to get rid of) in his mother's attic. Detective English called him in and told him there was an eye witness who saw him put it there. When Detective English told me that the man confessed when he said that, I was shocked.

"Are you kidding! There are no windows in that attic. How could he believe there was an eyewitness?!"

We laughed for a long time, just as I was inwardly laughing about suddenly knowing French.

"I would like to take you to lunch," was the jockey's next statement.

Our lunch was pleasant. Now he was curious. He dropped his attitude, and I gladly answered all his questions. When I connected through love and desire to help, it became easy to determine the feel of the images were not mine, they were coming from the chocolate filly standing in front of me. They were images of France. I sent back a thought of home and felt an overwhelming sadness in reply. Back and forth we went until some of the sadness was replaced with our friendship. As I write this, the spirit that lived in the body of the horse is helping me tell you what occurred. We have remained friends ever since, even long after she left this earth. I fell in love with her then, and knew, I always would feel her as a kindred spirit.

I would rather see horses roam together in their natural habitat. If I can help a horse live with something that I cannot change, then I will, so I go to paddocks at raceways, hoping that my love of their souls will help them through. While I left out how I felt about racing, by the time we finished lunch we were laughing and enjoying each other's gifts.

Phyllis' husband Kenny asked if I would go with him to another barn filled with racehorses. His horse seemed to be in trouble. When we arrived the man who was in charge was busy, so I asked if I could walk around and see all the horses in their stalls by myself.

"Sure."

That's all I needed. As I walked around I greeted most of them, then realizing I needed to get back to the men, I picked up speed and starting walking away from the stalls. A voice shouted within my mind: "I am the most successful horse here and you just passed me by." I looked at his name, M.L. I sent back through my mind a strong apology, and kept walking back to where Kenny and the owner of the place were waiting.

"Is M.L. a very successful horse?"

"He is the biggest winner by far," was the quick and firm response.

Did M.L. call out ? How? Please do not think I have the answer. My simple way of thinking goes like this: M.L. and I both have a natural translator ability that we don't shut down even when in trauma, so it is available to us even when most folks may not use theirs. Why did he sound offended, like someone with a need to be noticed? I thought that here was a horse who genuinely loved racing. He was into the sport like any athlete we've ever seen. I switched back to focusing on why I was asked to be there.

Having looked at the horse that Kenny asked me to take a look at and tell him my thoughts, I asked, "Can I see what you feed him please?"

I was given a two-inch cube-shaped piece of hay.

"The horse is sluggish, and now looking at the rest of the horses, I'll bet they are all a little sluggish."

"True."

"Can I see the package this comes in, please?"

Nothing was written on it to say why it was cube shaped.

My next idea was, "Please call the company and speak to the lab person in charge. Find out why it is cube shaped. It didn't just get that way."

Five minutes later we had the answer. They sprayed it with Bentonite! Total yikes! What were they thinking to feed a horse? Bentonite can be given to cows who are double ruminants. (Ruminants are the mammals that can digest cellulose from plants and chew the cud. The common examples of ruminant are cow and goat). We use it to bind with some toxins in our systems in detoxing. They stopped the cubes and all the horses regained their energy. Case solved.

Not being able to ride has never limited my desire or ability to be with horses. The chocolate filly is one of many horses I've spoken with over four decades. If I had let my fear of the unknown guide me, or my lack of intellectual knowledge of horses and their lives, I would never have met these wonderful gentle giants. Sue Ellen was a new client who came to my office. Her bag was laden with objects used by a horse she had recently acquired. Days later I received this email.

Dear Nancy,

(I had a session with you 3/23 evening and you spoke with Panache by touching his black halter.) Before coming to you, I was intimidated by Panache's size. You told me that my thoughts were smothering the power of my heart. I followed your instructions. After I said hello, I took him out of his stall and stood him in the center of the aisle. I stood by the right side of his head, slightly in front. I took the halter you held, and held it gently up against the left side of his face in a ball. With focused intention, I silently told him that you said hello again and again.

After 7 to 10 seconds, he lowered his head, and moved his muzzle into my chest and held it there. Then I snuggled him.

We've been friends ever since.

Sue Ellen

Dr. Ruth and I became friends through her love of horses. I had been teaching at a stable in Pennsylvania owned by Mike. Ruth was curious why Mike would hire a psychic, so she decided to visit when I was there. Ruth took notes and sent them to me. That began our decades-long friendship. Here are her notes:

We were at Mike's stable, and there was a little pony, a Hackney (the kind that pulls carts) with a lot of knee action. World champion, but wouldn't move right. Nancy looked at him and asked, "Where is your foot most comfortable?" He picked up a foot that had been pointing straight and turned it 45 degrees laterally. Then Buck knew how to shoe him and he was fine after that.

Then there was Mr. Majesty, the racehorse that Ronnie and Pete were going to sell for meat. Ronnie met Mike and convinced him to take Mr. Majesty. Before Mike could finish the deal, he agreed to let me call Nancy. We spoke on the phone and Nancy said to look at his kidneys. It was found that Mr. Majesty had a serious kidney infection and that's why he couldn't do anything. There were no overt symptoms, and the several veterinarians called in to look at Mr. Majesty had not considered a serious infection. After treatment he went on to win a handicap series at Penn National.

Years later, I called Nancy, because I had a patient who had some weird symptoms. She was in her early twenties, and had not slept more than an hour or two for years—constant headaches, muscle weakness, bedridden, and more. Tons of physicians looked yet no one had an answer. She immediately said, "The upper part of the spine is compressing the skull, by the brainstem." While she had many MRIs, none were specific for that region of the brain. I called the physician who was overseeing her situation. The MRI showed what Nancy described was true. The diagnosis was a Chiari malformation. The woman had surgery to correct it and within a matter of months was symptom free.

Watching Nancy easily slip into knowing horses I have loved, worked with, owned, and been friends with, rekindled my interest in the healing arts. A few years later, I pursued my dream of being an Osteopath. I opened a Wellness Center in Bedford, Pennsylvania. It incorporated my own devotion to the raising of awareness, the fine tuning of spiritual intention and intuition, and an occasional call to a dear friend who can sometimes find out what is going on with my human clients, by simply raising her level of awareness, to include the entire universe."

I was as shocked as Ruth was to know that what I saw led to a great relief for this young woman. I remember asking Ruth to spell the name of the problem, because I had never heard of it before. I am in awe of how our Creator instilled a mechanism in all of us that gives us the ability to see, hear and more, things that are beyond the obvious. The pineal gland receives the light wave, complete with universal information. Our pineal gland is loaded with optical receptors, just like our eyes. Light and dark transforms into images. We have a third eye, and not some imaginary thing made up—it is literal. Eastern thoughts about chakras are not made up.

Chakras[1] can be seen by many. They are the energetic field as it moves continually into dense matter. Horses have chakras, dogs have chakras, cats too, and all life has portals where the flow of energy can be seen by some of us. With practice, many come to feel the energy, sense it, see it, or simply believe in it, whether through science or philosophy.

Probably the most important lesson I'm still learning is to give time to make adjustments, to the exchange of energy information between myself and the other being. Waiting until I feel the spiritual connection. For me, it is an overwhelming feeling of love, enveloping all of us in a safe zone, where we can now communicate spirit to spirit.

If it is new to you, consider this. Create a quiet space; one where you can close your eyes and drift slowly into a relaxed state. If you need help, there are many guided meditations online. I have a few on my website in the blogs referring to a gift of music. While in this centered, deep breathing, relaxed state of mind, create an image, a belief, or a thought that you are an ancient and wise healer. You have learned the tradition passed down to you throughout the ages. Your energy becomes magically linked to the energy of the Creator. While the energy is always present, our commitment and belief focused on loving life, this is when we can become an instrument for peace, for love, for healing. Take any concern or worry you have for another species, whether it is for one specific friend or for one you have heard or read about. Place that particular being in the Light that is in your heart, flowing from the Divine to you, and then towards all. Stay there concentrating on that for as long as you can. Usually one to five minutes is fine. Everyone finds their own rhythm. Above all, leave the doubt and fears behind.

Every living being is created by the same Creator. All are instilled with the divine presence.

---

1 Chakra comes from the Sanskrit word, Muladhara, meaning wheel, and as translated from Hindi, it means wheel of spinning energy.

In 1976, I began to travel doing workshops throughout the United States. It was wonderful to meet so many good-hearted and fascinating people, yet I missed my children every moment. It led me to decide that I would give both them, and myself, a present each time. Years went by, and in December 2003, with my children successfully living on their own, I gave myself a gift for the holidays of two essential oils. I had joined a wonderful company, with like-minded folks who were environmentally aware, each seeking a toxin-free life. I started to learn the chemistry of essential oils, curious about how they had, in a short time, made such a huge difference to my body/mind. It was not the standard stuff we find at the stores and online. This was beyond anything I had encountered. I bought a reference book. Two blends stood out. Wondering how names of blends could support various emotional and mental needs, I decided these would be my holiday gifts to myself. Using these two new blends for supporting my daily gratitude prayer, magic did happen!

While I have loved doing a gratitude prayer most of my adult life, this one was a surprise. A drop of each of these oils suddenly led me to deeper feelings and thoughts about gratitude. Each morning for seven days the prayers were more and more intense. My thank you for the infinite light of love, compassion, kindness, healing energies, strength, and the ability to help many, were typical words I would say. Yet now it went into a feeling, that kept reaching higher for more intense love, intense gratitude, and everything became more alive. Noticing what my intention for the receiving of this infinite flow at its highest potential felt like, I was, and still am, connected to the All. To ancestors, to all existence here and beyond my knowing. Ecstatic, elated, and joyful are the feelings that began then and have not stopped. It made all the thoughts and books I read on frequency pale before the real experience of the shift into higher frequencies, and the ability to sustain them.

The first of several phone calls that were life-changing started on the seventh day. It was a subcontractor for Court TV. He was looking to do a few documentaries with me, about some of the crime cases I worked on with detectives. This would be early in January, for the first one, for a new series entitled "Psychic Detective." January, the month of no work usually, suddenly became exciting. Within a few hours, another call, this time from a New Jersey TV station. The producers of "To Your Natural Health" invited me to be a guest of Dr. DeSilva's program, where he would interview me. I hung up, thinking how amazing that January was now becoming a very interesting month for me! It did not stop there.

"Hi, Nancy, this is Mike."

Mike owns a stable where he trains show ponies. Being in Toronto, Canada, he had been calling for readings on the ponies for about fifteen years.

"Nancy, my partner has her farm in Virginia. She has fifty-six ponies there and would like you to visit, and to do your magic for a few days. Then I need you to fly up to my place. She will call you later today, when she gets back from the barn."

What just happened??? What was new in my life, that opened doors to new work? The oils! Nothing else was different. How, why, what, that's crazy. Yet it was true. It led me to dive into chemistry, go to the farms, the distilleries, attend any and all meetings where the founder would teach usage, chemistry, and so much more. I remember the thought at my first lesson, *I hit heaven and I am staying there.* That was, and is, my mantra since then.

Days later, I filmed the first of what was to be about eighteen shows for Court TV, Biography, A&E, the SiFi Channel, Paranormal Witness, the Nancy Grace Show, and more.

A week after filming the first show, I boarded a plane to head to Virginia. I decided to take a group of oils with me that I had learned were extremely useful for both humans and all other mammals. Another risk, since I had no idea what to do. I figured I would just apply them as I would on another person, same amount, roughly the same places. The woman who owns the stables is completely holistic in all she does. Organic food, generous heart, kind and loving with all the animals.

The ponies loved the oils, as did the dogs, who begged for more. Then when we were almost finished, I was asked to go with the owner to see a young pony. He was ten months old. When he was two months old, two older ponies attacked him. He had to have surgery to remove two destroyed ribs. Since then he refused to come out of his stall, and would shake when anyone was near him. I suggested we both apply one drop of a calming blend to our palms that I bought with me. We stood at the open door of the stall with palms up and simply stood quietly sending love. After a few minutes we walked slowly to the pony. I suggested we put our palms directly over the area of his side where the injury had occurred. Slowly lifting our palms and gently planting them on the pony, we both waited. Less than a minute went by when the pony let out a huge sigh and relaxed. After five or so minutes, we dropped our hands and began leaving the stall. The pony followed us. He went over to each person waiting and watching outside the stall. Sniffing each one, he then went over to the two adult ponies that were in stalls there.

Back home, and within days I flew up to Toronto. Mike and his family treated the ponies as extended family. The one that stands out for me is a miniature pony named Herbie. Herbie was eager to talk with me about every other pony that was there. He had comments on what he liked, what he disliked, who should do better. I nicknamed him Yenta (usually associated with "Fiddler on the Roof" as a Jewish woman who is a busybody). Herbie fit the profile.

Two and a half years later, Mike called to ask a brief question, about a pony who just won the nationals. I couldn't believe what I was hearing. It was the pony that had been injured. That pony has gone on to sire winner after winner, all loving the sport

While there are some horses and ponies who truly love to race, to show, and to be with humans, we can make life easier and more comfortable for all of those that would rather be running loose, by believing we can make a difference in the quality of their lives.

One particular standard-bred racehorse always brings a sadness to my heart. I was asked to see him, along with a request that I keep it confidential and show up directly at the barn, not the home. Intrigued, I arrived eager to find out what was so confidential. Seven people were in the barn, and one gorgeous horse oozing with power was in his stall. The folks simply said hi and asked that I take a look at him. I started my usual quieting down, sending love through my soul and got back a strong suggestion that if I came near him, I would not like the results. "Why?" I mentally sent back.

When I received his answer, I turned to the seven folks gathered: "I can't touch him, nor can any of you get into his stall and clean it, except for her."

I was pointing at one woman.

One man asked: "How do you know? And why is it? It's true, she is the only one who can do anything with him on a daily basis, except for the jockey, and he has trouble with him."

"Because he hates racing, racetracks and all that. She (pointing at the woman I mentioned) has never been to a racetrack. I have, and so have all of you."

"Yes, that's true. We hadn't thought of that."

I mentioned that I knew who the horse was. At the time, he was one of the most famous horses in our country. Even if anyone had no idea about racing, they knew the name of the horse.

"Why is it confidential? No worries, I promise not to tell. I am just curious."

"The owners refused to have someone come here, because they were afraid if word got out how difficult he is, the price would drop when they get stud fees and if they want to sell him."

Having a soul-to-soul meeting with the horse, I wanted him to know how helpless we all felt about his situation and wished for him better moments. Like us when we are feeling trapped, with no way out, he, despite his incredible abilities, was angry and terrified that he would never be free. I left wishing I could magically change his life for him. Maybe he felt it was all about money for these owners.

One of the first horses I worked with came about through moving to Budd Lake, New Jersey. Rebecca, almost 10 years old, and Jesse, age 4, both stated they wanted a dog. Off we went to an animal shelter. I heard from a few people about Alibi Acres. Susie was the owner of that shelter, and was wonderful with animals. It was a no-kill shelter.

Susie, a short blond woman, had a huge grin that matched her blue eyes dancing with delight at our interest in rescues. The dogs were all well taken care of; the cats ran loose in a barn-like setting, obviously used to getting lots of attention from her. She brought out a mutt with long brown hair, deep sad eyes, and the sweetest disposition. This little four-legged girl came over to us, fear spilling out of her eyes. Her movements showed that her body was hurting.

"She was abused and injured, and she now has seizures."

That's all we had to hear. She was ours. We named her Ramona, after a song from one of those black-and-white movies I love. Ramona proved to be a heroine. We poured our love into her. I researched natural ways to assist her, and she stopped having seizures. One day when we were out, burglars entered through my bedroom window. I wondered why they didn't go to any other room. In fact, I left the door to the bedroom open, and it was shut when we got home. Ramona had heard them and started barking. Not knowing she was an older disabled dog, they shut the door, took what they could, and left. They were so scared of the big bark that they left a fingerprint! The rest of that story is in my psychic detective book.

Through Susie, I met Marianne, a journalist, and a Society for the Prevention of Cruelty to Animals Agent. Our first meeting occurred in the early 1980s. Marianne was on the animal welfare board of Alibi Acres. The three of us, Marianne, Susie, and I, had all been working with horses, in one way or another. Marianne was writing for a statewide horse publication, as a reporter. She wanted to interview me for *The New Jersey Horseman*. She was looking to write it from the animal's point of view, which she hoped I could provide.

The horse she chose for the interview was Lad. Marianne had a special affinity for Lad, whose early history was filled with painful abuse. Lad had been with her for about a year, when I read him. I felt an instant easy communication, as if my mind, and his, spoke the same language. No need to spend any time interpreting my sensations or feelings, just flowing thoughts and words. I saw him winning ribbons, dozens of them; he did, indeed, go on to win every award he was eligible to win. Lad also told me about a piece of broken cartilage on the end of his nose. This had been broken, when his previous owner had twisted it while abusing him. Marianne had a vet check it, and he confirmed that it had been broken. It was so far up in his nose, that without knowing it was there, you would never have thought to look for it. Interestingly, a few years later, Lad competed against a horse that belonged to the man who Marianne had bought Lad from, the man who had been Lad's abuser.

Marianne told Lad, "You know what you're going to do? You're going to beat that S.O.B."

And so he did. Lad had been 200 pounds underweight due to neglect and physical abuse, and also terrified of men when he first was sold to Marianne. Her love broke the circle of hate and fear, and wove magic, as Lad became an outstanding champion with his partner. Marianne's rapport with Lad became the Zen experience of being one with each other. She could hear him talking in her head. She had conversations with him all the time, and knew what he was going to do before he did it. He became spectacular in the show ring. Lad told me he would live to be twenty-eight to thirty years old. Last I spoke with Marianne, he was twenty-seven and in excellent health.

Maniac was Marianne's Himalayan, long-hair cat, and at the time he was, according to her, "the biggest slob that ever walked." He would not keep himself clean, and he hated to be bathed. He had a coat that looked like, "who did it and ran."

Underneath the mess, I saw a winner. After a moment's introduction to Maniac, I told Marianne, "Someday you are going to show that cat." She laughed. Seven years later, when Maniac was twelve years old, he became Double Supreme National Household Pet. He went into the show ring for the first time, at nine years of age. Gradually, he began to groom himself impeccably, and become very proud of his appearance.

Because of my friendship with Marianne, I volunteered to help on several cases of animal abuse. In the mid-1980's, the SPCA agents of Morris County were dealing with extreme cases of animal cruelty, such as ritual killings and cockfights. Then there was the case that made headlines.

The neighbors of a family that had two great danes complained that the dogs had disappeared but their collars and chains were still there. They accused the family of killing their dogs. Marianne called me. I told her the owner's son did it, and they were buried in the backyard in plastic bags. I warned her to watch out for him, as he was very disturbed and dangerous.

"The mother will answer the door, and the son will be listening from the top of a flight of stairs with a shotgun," was the image I conveyed.

Marianne took my advice and went in with a police officer. When they arrived at the house, the mother answered the door. The son was listening from the top of a flight of stairs, and he was holding a shotgun. The officer called for backup. They arrested the son for threatening an officer of the law. Once she felt safe, the mother showed them where in the backyard where to dig. They found the bodies of the two dogs.

The mother knew her son had shot the dogs, but did not report it. She had been in constant fear of her son. He was prosecuted, and in the end, the court ordered psychiatric help for the boy. The probable cause for the boy's behavior, it was found, was severe child abuse by his father, early in life. What if we all see something, and do something? Getting help for those who show signs of severe mental anguish, by abusing the innocent who cannot fight back, can only happen when we all make a difference.

Around the same time, I was looking out my window. I viewed a neighbor's teenage son Bob. He was walking over to their next door neighbor's dog, who was on a run. I witnessed him hit the dog. He then walked back to his home. I called him and demanded he come right over to my home. Knowing I worked with the police, he came right over.

How to get his attention? I put some rock music on then answered the door. Surprised by the music, he said he liked what I was playing.

"I wrote it, now sit down" I pointed at a chair for him.

After our talking ranged from music to his having a father who was a violent drunk who no longer lived with them, he promised to try to find better outlets for his frustration. About a year later, I was asked to look at a robbery of jewelry. Up he came in my mind. I called the detective I worked with. Bob was picked up, along with the jewelry he had in a bag. He was sent to juvenile detention. He was allowed one phone call. He called me. My only thought was, he had learned to swallow his anger until he couldn't stand it, and then would impulsively act out, causing a cascade of trouble for him and all around. That incident, and so many more, tell me we need to help when they are young, not wait until it's so late that they may be beyond redemption. The problem is recognized in the book *Ghosts from the Nursery: Tracing the Roots of Violence*, by Meredith S. Wiley and Robin Karr-Morse. So far the solution has evaded us.

When abuse occurs, it has a rippling effect. Whether we send loving energy to those hurting, call it in to the agency that can do some good, or get directly involved, we need to feel useful. We feed our own souls by connecting to the highest frequency, for the highest good for all. I've sent love beams to others when I lay paralyzed, knowing that my soul still needs to be useful to all. While the body may be far from perfect, the soul is always beautifully strong. The solution is within us all.

Back in 1984, I had at least four years of working regularly with animals. That year, a call came from Jim, a trainer I had met through a wonderful couple, Marlene and Galen. I had been giving them readings and assessing the ponies they were training. They were two of the more dedicated and caring animal owners I have ever run across. Galen had gone on to teach many other people healing techniques to use on people and animals and, when last we spoke, was helping many with his use of several healing modalities. We definitely thought alike about techniques, and knew to keep in mind that what works for one doesn't necessarily help another.

It was a beautiful autumn morning, a perfect day for a long drive into Pennsylvania horse country. The drive made the day more like a holiday in the country, not work. Work is a funny word, rich with meaning. I love Joseph Campbell's thought, "Follow your bliss." He saw it as an essential part of the formula for living life to the fullest. I've learned that even in the toughest moments, while looking at a fresh crime scene or hearing the wailings of a male horse when his best friend and love, a female horse, died, I need to find a coping mechanism. I now rely on my belief in the flow of spirit that connects us all. I love entering into as high a state of love as possible, hoping it cascades and encircles the grieving parties here along with those who are adjusting to the other side.

The roads were lined with blazing fall colors everywhere, the leaves readying to enter into a new state of existence where they would rejoin with all. It was an awesome journey that reminded me of what we all go through. The directions were easy, hardly any turns, until I got to their town. Two hours of solitude and I was ready for people. Even this introvert likes to climb out of her shell.

Jim came striding to the car, with a gait created from thousands of hours on horses. He had long, lean muscles; hair that never looked combed, and eyes that showed he had one focus and one focus only—horses. In all the times I spent working with Jim, I never got to know him except for his concern for the animals in his care.

"Hi Jim, thanks for the directions. They were perfect."

As I pulled up, Jim was all questions and nervousness.

"How many people can follow you about? Are the owners permitted to be there? We've got about eleven horses for you to see."

"Jim, as long as everyone can fit in the barn, it doesn't matter to me who or how many people show up. Just please tell everyone not to discuss the animals out loud until I've worked on them."

When I am on an assignment for an animal, it is no different than any other work I do. It's easier for me to work cold. I can deep dive into the universal connection without any preconceptions. If I know too much ahead of time, my conscious mind can take over. I need to connect with the animal, soul to soul, establishing a strong bond between us, so that the truth of where we each come from is mutually understood. Once I've done what I can, then I can hear other input.

They were ready for me. There must have been two dozen people, a half-dozen dogs, and an unknown number of cats all curious about the newcomer. A dog ran up to greet me. I love animals; they have a way of making me feel welcome, as if they can still feel the shy little girl present in me. Like many folks, it's easier to trust all other species since their instincts seem to be sharper about who to be friends with.

"Let me introduce you to everyone." Jim was eager to get started.

Introductions done, a glass of water in hand, someone carrying a tape recorder as we started down towards the first stall Jim had chosen for me to enter. In the stall was a big, beautiful chestnut male, with a star on his forehead. He was taller than average and more muscular. The name on the stall read Flying King.

"Hello," my mind sent. "I'm here to be with you anyway that will help. Please show me what you need. I love you."

My head went reeling with pain. I almost fell over in the grip of shooting knife-like pain that was all over my head. Migraines! My God, how horrible. This horse had gripping waves of head pain, which kept him both furious and scared. Tears welled up in me. How could he not be crazy, that poor soul. My hands became charged with my feelings of concern. My whole being became dedicated to helping him be free of his misery. I sent this thought: "God, please bring through me whatever powers of healing and love that will aid in the most loving way possible, for this soul, known as Flying King who waits for help." Then I waited to feel it was time.

My hands felt warmer than they had a moment ago, my fingers were tingling. Gently I placed my hands on the left side of his back. Moving my hands slowly, I listened carefully for what they could tell me. Images of a network of energy floated before me. Like a grayish-blue gauze that has depth and motion to it, I watched it vibrate beneath my hands. Wherever it showed itself as twisted, or I heard or felt a discordant rhythm to the energy, I would leave my hands over the sight. I asked for God's Light to pass through me into my friend. About a half hour later, my hands were massaging and gently pressing the top of his head. His eyes were droopy and relaxed. I sensed a realignment take place in my image of his cranial sutures. My hands walked down to the right jaw, massaging with my fingers, more and more vigorously, and then his left jaw. He rested his head on my shoulder, gently nudging me. Sending, "I love you too, you sweetie," I responded. We were in complete empathy, mutually open and trusting. Powerful rushes of love poured through me as we kept the cycle going.

Not moving from our circle of light, I asked, "Can I have a brush, please?"

A moment later, a brush appeared from the crowd. My desire to brush his mane sent shivers down my right arm into my fingertips. As I held the brush, I lost all sense of separation. My fingers, the brush, and the mane were joined as one. Long strokes of the brush seemed to relax him. The brush became a bridge of love, a conduit between horse and woman. His eyes followed me with curiosity. Again I sent a thought, "I'm just brushing your beautiful mane. I hope you're feeling better."

Gradually I looked up and noticed no one had moved. Flying King was almost asleep with his head on my shoulder. I was so engrossed in our reverie, I could not discern their expressions, only that they looked strange. I wondered what was wrong..

"Anybody care to say something, ask something?"

Jim was the first, "How did you do that?"

"Do what?"

Jim continued, "No one has been able to touch his head since we've had him. All he would do was bite and kick. Couldn't even brush his mane."

"How long has it been?"

"Three years," was someone in the crowd's response.

"I guess if I had the equivalent of a migraine for three years, I'd be pretty nasty. Matter of fact, when I have chronic pain there is a particular word most people could use to describe me. It rhymes with witch."

Although that is no longer the case when I am in pain, it definitely was in moments of anger when up came the memories of the betrayals by some humans who caused my injuries. It was also the inspiration to completely enter a holistic lifestyle along with learning lots of techniques to release stored negative emotions.

The rest of the day was simple. Flying King had helped me show the people what I do. They were easier to work with after that. I worked on ten more horses, none as troubled as King. Everyone was eager to help their own horse. One woman asked if I would look at a dog that was having some problems. With a heaping does of ethics, humility, and gratitude, the recipe of caring for all lifts us up. When we said good-bye, I ran back to kiss King one more time, and to thank him for letting me be a part of his life. We are friends for life and beyond. A few days later, the trainer called to tell me he could brush the horse's mane for the first time. Weeks later, he told me the horse had become increasingly affectionate and easy to work with.

A strange twist occurred. A reporter from a horse magazine called and wanted references. I gave her a few names to call, among them Flying King's owner. The owner refused to speak, telling the reporter that she would not want it known that her horse ever had a problem, as the price for resale could go down. I always felt sad knowing that it was more important to keep high money value on an animal than to care to help others in the same boat.

If you love animals, you probably already practice some sort of method of sending love. Beginners are those who have not considered themselves capable of helping someone furry, feathered, finned, scaly or any other species. Focused intention matters, along with the understanding you are not opening up your personal energy, even for your own kin. You are tapping into the universal life force, using the energy that sustains us all. Over the last forty-five years of teaching, I have watched beginners of laying on of hands with comments such as "I didn't feel anything, I'm lost," "My hands are hot and tingly, it was amazing," "I'm not sure; it felt nice, the person I was working with said her shoulder was in pain before we started and now the pain is gone."

Every day I talk and lay gentle hands on Audrey, a huge philodendron plant, now over forty years of age. She was a small lady with three leaves, and now she is constantly showing new babies. Love is truly the universal language.

In the book *Healers and Healing*, published in 1989, there is a common thread for all healers. Well-known healers of those times stated that it isn't their need to help someone else, as much as their need to stay connected to the oneness. Be a safe haven that believes in possibilities. A mixture of prayerful concentration of one's own connection to the divine flow of healing energy, and our desire to be of service, lifts us up to feel the truth. I believe we can all be great healers.

Hidden within our daily lives, is the potential for great happenings.

It all begins with our beliefs.

While camping out in the West around Utah, I met two young men who were also camping. They had just encountered their first rattlesnake. Tim had gone up the trail first, and halfway up, about six feet in front of him, mad as hell, was a rattler, rattling away. Tim's heart raced faster standing still than it ever had running. He decided he had no chance so he might as well gamble on becoming friends. This all happened in about two minutes. While Tim did not know rattlers well, he was intelligent, knew something about snakes, could hear the rattle, and knew what a striking pose looked like. Instead of running, Tim kneeled down, "to make myself non-threatening," and spoke to the snake, calling him brother and friend. He said that all the while he was talking he was sending pictures of what he believed was friendship. He couldn't be sure of how long, and it did feel like hours, but his buddy said it was only a few minutes later that the rattler bid them farewell and left them alone on the trail.

What about these wonderful, heroic animals who do all kinds of rescue, even at the cost of their own lives? Certainly they can sense our needs. We need to sense theirs.

The lesson Tim taught me was wonderful and simple:

When fear does not guide us, our hearts can lead us home.

The evolution of trusting our intuition, no matter how psychic we are, can be a difficult task. Anytime we have been scolded, ridiculed, or ignored as a result of attempting to apply an idea, we may have absorbed a message that our intuition and creativity can get us in trouble. Enough of that; we have to undo the problem, recover the trust, and use our intuition. What happened for me with the French horse and jockey was the perfect mixture of antagonism, happiness at a new discovery, and rebelliousness (mine, in case that's not obvious), and a tiny drop of annoyance (which was also mine). Stirred together, I was able to make the leap into "knowing."

That doesn't mean I was sure of what came through. It does mean that I didn't care about the risk of being foolish or wrong.

Using your imagination, or clairvoyantly seeing what occurs, clairaudient hearing, or any of the psychic sensing, feel the energy of your prayers, wishes, and thoughts flow outward toward the heart of the other being. It does not matter how large or small the being is. Love is the greatest power for the highest good for all.

Creativity comes into play here. Depending on what you want to happen, you might send a request, never a command. Sit back, relax, enjoy, and visualize. You may want to gather photos of animals you love. They may no longer be on earth, or they may be lying at your feet. Sit quietly, and when you know that you are as relaxed as you can get, hold one of the photos in your hands. Let yourself float gently, as if you are gliding on a lake that glimmers with placidity.

Converse with the pet in the photo. Give yourself plenty of time to feel or hear a response. Rushing through this exercise closes the door to the information. Fear of what you may or may not find, acts to create a chemistry that closes off the information. After a few minutes, open your eyes and stay quiet. Mentally converse with the friend in the photo. Imagination is key. That's where we playfully open up. Do this many times, and you will become comfortable with this newfound skillset. When you feel like exploring further, ask your friends for photos. One cautionary note: It is important to believe in yourself, and also to be graciously tactful. If you believe you are picking up information that is frightening or uncomfortable, take it inside yourself. Send the information to the Divine Light, ask God for the right words, the right tone, the right way of handling, and then share. Getting feedback is important along with keeping notes on what you are doing.

Chapter 7

All Animals are my Teachers

Sometimes the inevitable is truly the inevitable. Terry and Casey were inseparable. Casey was dying. Terry stayed home from work, to minister and be with her beloved friend, who happened to be a dog. She asked me to take a look at Casey. Casey was about 20 pounds of pure love.

Casey was an incredibly easy conversationalist, despite his ebbing energy. He lay on a couch with Terry at his side. Casey and I mentally conversed.

"I'm not in any pain. I'm leaving within days."

"Is there anything I can do for you, Casey?"

"Tell mommy I was with her before, and I'll be with her again. The dog before me was not as close to her. Mommy and I have been together several times. We have grown so close."

"Terry, Casey claims not to be in pain, is at most, days from leaving this earth, and is quite ready. Did you have a dog before Casey? Casey says you were not as close to the other."

"That would be Charlie. No, Casey is special, very special. He's my best *friend*. We have an incredible bond."

Casey turned to me and relayed: "Tell her I love the photos she took of me. Particularly, how I got ready for them."

Perplexed, I repeated the statement. I've learned that some of the oddest things I get are the most accurate. Terry laughed, got up, and walked over to a mantle where some photos stood.

"I dressed Casey up in sunglasses, bandanas, hats, and other props. Casey always looked forward to it."

When I left, it was clear that although the journey without Casey's presence would be hard, Terry had an amazing relationship that would live in her heart forever. If someone you know is worried about a pet, leap in with your heart and soul. Follow your instincts. Trust yourself, trust the wisdom that pours through all of life. Perhaps your desire to be of service will lead you to discover how powerful your own gifts are. Although it can be painfully sad, helping the innocent leave, and supporting those left here on earth, is great karma. Having lived with close friends as they were leaving this earth for their next journey, and given sermons at their memorial celebration of their lives; having buried many a furry friend, and keep their memories alive in my heart; I know that one of the gentlest loving feelings is helping a friend move on to their next journey. Then there are those far away, who I never met face to face, who have shared some beliefs, like Maya Angelou, Anwar Sadat, Ghandi, and so many more, who have helped me continue to love all, even when I can't stand them! I've found that I can despise an action, not a soul. A dolphin who was deeper in his belief opened more of my heart.

The weekend I moved to Budd Lake, New Jersey, I also went down to Princeton University. I was to give a workshop for the American Holistic Psychology Association. They assigned a man to help and escort me around the campus.

"Hi, I'm Steve McGruder."

That began a lifelong friendship. Steve travels the world, and one of the places he went to for years (he pops up every few years in New Jersey for a visit) was the coast of Wales. One day while visiting my home, he pulled out a photo of a dolphin.

"His name is Percy, can you get any message from him?"

I can still feel what transpired with Percy. When I tune in, I put aside all the usual questions: how does this work, can I do this, what if I don't get anything? I know I can't do justice with words, yet I attempted to, when Steve asked me what happened. A few years later, I had the delightful task of writing it as lyrics for a children's song. Elaine Silver, folk singer, wrote the music along with eleven other songs we wrote over six weeks. Here are the lyrics, told to me by Percy.

> Percy the Dolphin comes to the bay, a truly gifted spirit reveals a special way
>
> He gave our world a message early one day
>
> And here's a vision he asked me to relay
>
> You are young inhabitants on our Mother Earth
>
> Our matriarchal waters we have thanked since birth
>
> Many other species we've watched coming through
>
> Removing one another they also thought they knew
>
> Percy the Dolphin came to the coast of Wales
>
> To guide us with a light, to share an ancient tale
>
> The story that he tells us, the truth that he unveils
>
> Brings to us a heritage proclaiming to prevail
>
> Percy the Dolphin sends us all his love
>
> Universal energies below and from above
>
> Says to know that mother watches patiently
>
> And waits for her children to live peacefully
>
> You are young inhabitants on your Mother Earth

Our matriarchal waters we have thanked since birth

Be assured our planet has and will endure

Eons old the Alchemist, her light is truly pure

Percy the Dolphin sends us all his love.

– From the collection "Songs of the Spirit," co-written by
Elaine Silver and Nancy O. Weber, copyright 1987

I remember the feeling of Percy laughing and suggesting that like a human teenager, our species can be a problem to ourselves and all others. The feelings he relayed were more than any words I can share. I was elated, knowing that other species were so kind and compassionate towards a species where so many can apparently turn on its own. I once read that if you survive an earthquake, tsunami, hurricanes, tornadoes, and such, the trauma experienced, however severe, is not as severe as when your own species attacks you. Even dolphins have their moments of aggression; most of it is the male population towards the female, and competing with other males during mating season. Was Percy saying some things do not change? All I know is, when I am upset at the human race I think of what he said. We are at a teenage state of human evolution. What if we can enter true adulthood? Where kindness, compassion, and love for one's own life, and for all life, is throughout the species. The only way I can use those thoughts, is to keep to what I feel is authentic love towards self, and all others. Then my world view has sweeter thoughts, with patience, loving hues, and tone.

When it comes to problems, the attitude we take determines the outcome. Here's someone who learned to adapt to circumstances, and have fun with stretching into the unknown. Christina is blind; Regal, her seeing eye dog, was lying at her feet when Christina sat in one of my animal communication classes. I was handing out envelopes; each one contained a photo of an animal I knew.

"How am I supposed to work with a photograph?" Christina wanted to know.

"No one gets to see what is in the photo; all of your classmates have their photos in envelopes too. No one can open them until after we work; at that time I will assist you."

The photo I handed Christina was of Beauty, the mourning dove we raised. Concentrating on quieting her chatter, and just allowing herself to feel the energy emanating from the photo, Christina did as I asked.

When it came her turn, like many others she remarked, "I don't know, I couldn't possibly really know anything. I thought some things, and here is the thought that popped up. First, it was of a bird. I don't know what kind, an uncommon rescue and a release."

Could she be any more accurate? I doubt it. Christina was thrilled. She went on to use her abilities, and related that it helped her discover that she could use this newfound gift to explore the outer world in a way she had never considered before. Many people discover when you remove the distractions, and you can't use the excuse of body language, what's left is that invisible metaphysical universe of mind, thought, and spirit. Your turn. Start recording your instant flashes and you will learn to trust them.

Look around your dwelling, find letters, note cards, and objects others have given you. Sit down with a notebook or recorder at your side. Take each item and hold it, while you enter a quiet, meditative state. Observe your thoughts, feelings, ideas. If words pop up, notice them; if images come to you, note them too. Date and record all your findings. When you are ready, check out your findings.

Knowing how I felt when I first began to control these wild gifts, I adore watching others find their way deep inside, letting their souls take over completely. I love being their cheerleader. Once I became drenched in the wonder of the universal connection between all of life, I was able to see how children start out knowing that. Too often children need to protect themselves. The situations we encounter as young ones may suppress our gifts, or develop them into strong antennas, hoping to control what the next moment holds. Same with many other species. Sometimes it brings a desire to protect the innocent. One woman I met when I went to an animal shelter was just that. She was all about rescuing and loving all domesticated animals. Her shelter was where I went to get our first rescue in New Jersey. Ramona was a wonderful mixed-breed canine. Broken hip, epilepsy, and yet the sweetest precious lady that became my assistant in solving a burglary! I've written about this wonderful canine in my previous book on being a psychic detective.

I had just finished reading *The Tracker,* by Tom Brown, Jr, when Susie (the owner of the shelter) called me frantically. She had agreed to temporarily host a Chincoteague pony named King Neptune. He was meant to go to someone she knew and they were away for the week.

On the way to put King Neptune in her barn, he escaped. On the phone, I suddenly had a vision of this pony. Not knowing if it was true or not, I went ahead and told her what I saw.

"I see him near a swamp, and looking for water, he's deep inside woods. Miles from you. The only person who can actually help get him is the tracker, Tom Brown. He will need his crew. They would need to do a round-up. When they do get him and bring him back, you will see that some of his fur will grow back in gray where the brambles has scratched and removed the fur."

Susie called Tom Brown, who called his crew. They traveled into the woods where there was a swampy area, and found King Neptune, who tried to run away. They were ready and their round-up captured him. His legs had patches of gray fur.

Synchronicity began when I bought the book *The Tracker*. Looking back at the thread that brought King Neptune back to the barn, I wondered then, and still do, was my soul knowing the need to remember Tom Brown for someone else? Having read the book, I saw he lived in New Jersey about an hour from Susie's home. Buying a book doesn't always mean I read it right away. This one I read nonstop soon after I got home. My children were at school, no clients until evening meant I could read. It was a quick read; was that luck? The call came within days. Tom Brown traveled the U.S., and sometimes outside it when called on to track missing people. He was home. For me, it means we are all connected, and the universal rhythm matches the personal rhythm of need to have something happen. The ability to get anything done when there is more than one being involved, requires a universal agreement with the source, the Creator, whatever we each consider is the creator of all life, here and beyond. That to me is synchronicity: Everyone at the same time is there for the higher good of all.

Nancy, King Neptune and Susie

Chapter 8

A Fish and Water Mammals are my Teachers

In 1968, Gil and I moved to 410 Calle Norzagaray in Old San Juan, Puerto Rico. Knowing we would be going to take a course in scuba diving, I decided to read the Navy's book of research on sharks. That was a big mistake. I became nervous about going to open waters. Finished with the course, we went to Fajardo, where the navy base was along the coast. Taking a boat out to open waters, and jumping in, was exciting. I love water and felt right at home, except for one noticeable issue. I kept checking the waters for sharks. Suddenly I saw three manta rays swim past me, and in the opposite direction, swimming past me a moment later, were three barracuda! They seemed to say "Welcome to our world." I took a deep breath of gratitude, figuring they felt fairly safe, so why wouldn't I? That did it. I spent many hours watching beautiful paintings by our Creator of plants, fish and light known as the Caribbean Sea.

Having lived in Old San Juan, Puerto Rico for two years, I felt drawn to all that lived in the waters. Jumping forward, I married Dick Weber February 11, 1989 (my birthday), and three years later, we were invited by close friends to fly down to their fifty-three foot, all electric winch sailboat in St. Thomas. We sailed straight to the British Virgin Islands. That is where I fell in love with a little fish.

We anchored about half a mile from Big Dog Island, a favorite snorkeling area for folks from all over the world. This uninhabited island is rich with coral reefs and fish. Our friends decided to rest on the boat while we went snorkeling.

Knowing my husband I commented, "Dick, you are not used to snorkeling. We need to be buddies in the water, no wandering off from each other, OK?"

I think he muttered. Dick was used to going off on his own explorations on land. Off we went, and when he attempted, without gloves, to touch an appealing reddish coral, I grabbed his hand and shook my head firmly NO. Fire coral! It can burn like a hot fire. Suddenly I could feel him freeze up. He was in a panic. Knowing how quickly any species can sense the fear, I felt action was necessary. I tapped him to follow me. He pointed at a barracuda that was about two feet in length. I nodded, and tapped him again to follow me. Since he was about six years old he was legally blind without glasses. I thought wearing only goggles, his vision of the barracuda was distorted and frightening. I sent a prayer up to help me help him. A yellow fish no bigger than my pinky tapped me on my nose, and started aiming for open waters. I followed with Dick right behind me. The fish led us back to the boat! It's funny, I trusted the fish to know what we needed. Fish do not normally leave their own territory. Dick raced up the few steps into the boat telling me to hurry. Instead, I stayed by the boat with the fish letting me pet her/him. Then it tapped my nose, and went back to home turf. When Dick tells the story, the barracuda grows to about six feet. When I tell it, the Yellow Fish is the hero.

From my friend, the Yellow Fish as small as my pinkie to our cousin Tommy's wild encounter in the deep waters of the Atlantic, seems a fitting way to say to you that friendship is everywhere.

Tommy is a retired Navy Seal. He told me of his encounter in deep waters of the Atlantic Ocean. As a Navy Seal, he was dropped from a helicopter into the Atlantic Ocean for twenty minutes. A test for the "just in case," if a plane or helicopter needed time to rescue. Within a minute he was surrounded by humpback whales. They stayed with him for the twenty minutes he hung out in the vast ocean, and did not leave until he was safely picked up and back in the helicopter. Consider what they understood, how quickly they acted, and how loving they are.

Having lived in the Caribbean and now in the Northeast, I went to Cape Cod, Massachusetts for whale watching. It was announced that a fin whale mother and baby came to the left side of the boat. All the folks ran to that side. It became so crowded, I didn't attempt to see what was going on. I went to the right side, and sent a focused thought filled with love. "Namaste, beloved kin. I pray that you and your child have a healthy, beautiful life ahead of you for many years. You have blessed us with your presence." Opening my eyes, I saw mom and her baby staring at me! I heard folks asking "Where did they go." It is a profound blessing to know I was heard by the innocent.

> *How it is that animals understand things I do not know, but it is certain that they do understand. Perhaps there is a language which is not made of words and everything in the world understands it. Perhaps there is a soul hidden in everything and it can always speak, without even making a sound, to another soul.* —Frances Hodgson Burnett

Thank you for your interest and love of other species. Whether it is your dog, cat, hamster, gerbil, horse, bird, or any other living being that is not human, you and I wish for a more innocent world, filled with compassion for all of them. Below are some helpful resources. If you pass this book to friends, or to your library, be sure to add to the list of resources, particularly if you have any shelters local to you.

Resources

Infinite Possibilities

When I self-published The Life of a Psychic Detective, I promised myself to donate $1 from each sale to Hope for Justice, a partner in the D. Gary Young Living Foundation. For this book, I am donating one book to animal shelters for every ten sold.

Animal Scents University is an in-depth resource for non-branded essential oil education. Susan Albright, DVM (lucky me she wrote my forward), and Kate Brown, CCA (Certified Clinical Aromatherapist) created this resource. You can check it out at https://www.animalscentsu.com/ Lightwingcenter.

As a Certified Clinical Aromatherapist, I created certification courses on the use of essential oils for lay practitioners and CEs for nurses. More information is at Lightwingcenter.org.

There are many strays and injured animals. If you are on social media you may find folks with gofundme sites to support shelters and vet bills for injured homeless animals. Check the name of the veterinarian or animal hospital for authenticity.

Fund raisers for local shelters. Most shelters have a wish list of needs. Towels, pet food, and more. If you volunteer, great. If you would rather gift the shelter, think of asking for their wish list. Many of my friends also offer some of our favorite essential oil blends to assist the animals that have gone through so much. Reach me by email through my website nancyorlenweber.com for any info on what to use. I'm happy to help. Old towels, kitty litter, and food, food, food are always useful. Please check with your local shelter for their specific needs beforehand.

www.avma.org is the American Veterinary Medical Association. This is a great resource to find a vet who does acupuncture and uses more natural products, which may include Chinese herbs, essential oils, and supplements along with the usual tests.

At nancyorlenweber.com, clicking on the button "Essential Oils" takes you to the network market I have used since 2003. It embeds my member ID 835516. My favorite thought when finding this company is "I hit heaven and I am staying there." My first nursing teacher, in 1961, taught us about a holistic lifestyle. Young Living embodies that for me. I am always happy to help anyone learn more about these products and how to use them. If you are not using them yet, you may want to chat with me or email a query. Besides being helpful to us, they are as important for the sake of all our pets.

Reiki, absent healing, or any other energy healing can be of use for your pets. The best resource is our loving hearts reaching out to those closest to us, and then to the world. Enjoy stretching your abilities to communicate? Seek local or online classes with animal communicators. I know there are many who love to share and educate. My online classes are at my website.

Other healing modalities are, Intuitive Touch Animal Care with Anne Angelo Webb for healing work, and the Tellington Touch. There are so many more, but these are the ones I am most familiar with.

Lastly and most importantly, know you can do it too! We all start somewhere. Keep a written or voice-recorded account of your conversations with all your other species buddies. It helps to be able to look back and see how your abilities grow over time. It is a wondrous blessing to know any of our friends from other species on a soul-to-soul basis.

From my heart to yours, thank you for sharing this journey,

—Nancy